kirigami

ACKNOWLEDGMENTS

My thanks go to the following firms and shops which placed their material at my disposal; it was used for the photographs in the various chapters on the types of paper and tools: Bellomi srl (Via Lomellina 64, Milan) for the tools and for graphic design.
The two Valli International srl (Via Combattenti 4, Borgo Sesia) for the original paper deriving from villages in India.
Paper srl (Via San Maurilio 4, Milan) for the various cotton papers and those with fiber inserts.
I would also like to thank all those who have been particularly helpful with their advice, their availability, and the support given me on this occasion, as on others.

Library of Congress Cataloging-in-Publication Data Available

10 9 8 7 6 5 4 3 2 1

First paperback edition published in 2001 by
Sterling Publishing Company, Inc.
387 Park Avenue South, New York, N.Y. 10016
First published in Italy by RCS Libri S.p.A.
© 1999 by RCS Libri S.p.A.
English translation © 2000 by Sterling Publishing Co., Inc.
Distributed in Canada by Sterling Publishing
℅ Canadian Manda Group, One Atlantic Avenue, Suite 105
Toronto, Ontario, Canada M6K 3E7
Distributed in Great Britain and Europe by Cassell PLC
Wellington House, 125 Strand, London WC2R 0BB, England
Distributed in Australia by Capricorn Link (Australia) Pty. Ltd.
P.O. Box 704, Windsor, NSW 2756 Australia
Printed in China

Sterling ISBN 0-8069-4490-0 Trade
             0-8069-4454-4 Paper

Laura Badalucco

kirigami

Sterling Publishing Co., Inc.
New York

CONTENTS

INTRODUCTION

A cut and a fold are all it takes to transform a plain sheet of paper into a three-dimensional object ù a tree, a cloud, a fish. Creating an entire world with a single sheet of paper is not, after all, that difficult. The kirigami technique – the Japanese craft of cutting paper (Kiri = to cut, Gami = Kami = to fold) – is at the basis of this new experience. Learning this craft will allow you to make figurative or abstract three-dimensional models from a single sheet of paper by means of an accurate system of cuts and folds.

Objects will take shape by simply opening and closing a sheet of paper, giving particular prominence to the relationship between spatial and temporal dimensions. But that's not all: by simply looking at, or feeling, a sheet of paper, it will itself suggest what it could become, transmitting different visual, tactile, olfactory sensations according to its different nature. Loving paper, then, is at the root of this craft and it is perhaps the only commitment that will be asked of you.

In the Far East, paper has been valued and admired for its varied qualities ever since ancient times.

Three-dimensional paper forms were already widely used in the early Chinese and Japanese Buddhist temples, as votive offerings to the gods. It is still common practice among Shintoists today to lay folded and cut paper shapes on the ropes that mark off trees or rocks — these last considered sacred because they are believed to be imbued with divine presence.

During the Edo period in Japan, that is, between the 17th and 19th centuries, cutting and folding paper became a full-fledged art, very similar to, though differing from, Origami (the craft of folding paper). Similarly, in the West, books with movable elements already existed in the 13th century, made with cut, folded, and even glued paper. Today these books are called pop-ups and are used mainly in illustrated children's books.

In the 1920s and 1930s, Joseph Albers introduced the study of three-dimensional paper and cardboard models into the core Bauhaus course, in order to induce his students to think in terms of space. This concept still exists in the Basic Design courses taught in many design schools, and inspired the "traveling sculptures" that Bruno Munari designed towards the end of the 1950s. These are pocket sculptures made from a single piece of paper, cut and folded with a technique that is very similar to kirigami. Currently, kirigami has inspired the development of expressive new techniques in both the East and the West.

This book is divided into four sections: Technique, Projects, Objects and Templates. The first section will teach you the basics of the craft, the outcome of a crossover between kirigami and other dry-paper crafts; it will also help you to recognize the characteristics of the different kinds of paper available and to use them to your advantage, as well as help you to experiment with your own versions of the projects presented.

Be particularly careful when letting children make these models. Specifically designed variations (described at length in another manual) are used to teach children the art of kirigami. These suggest using, among other things, scissors rather than a cutting knife.

Once you have learned all there is to know about kirigami, you will be able to create a whole series of both abstract and figurative projects, as well as a host of interesting decorative objects. Projects and objects have been grouped together under themed headings (abstract, architecture, birthday invitations). Every group is made up of increasingly complex projects, and every set is more difficult than the previous one but less complex than the next. If you intend to select at random the models you would like to make, without following the order set out in this book, remember to check the number of asterisks ascribed to your chosen project. Every model, in fact, has been graded according to the level of cutting and folding difficulty, ranging from one asterisk for the easier projects to three for the more complex ones.

To begin with, we suggest you use the materials and procedures indicated in our instructions. As soon as you feel relatively confident with these, try using other types of paper and experimenting with the procedures: there is no better way than this to discover the world in a single sheet of paper.

TECHNIQUE

PAPERS AND CARDS

White card

Colored card weighing (160 gr)

All projects presented in this book are made exclusively with paper.

Before making the models, you will have to decide on the shape, color, properties, weight, and texture of the paper. While choosing a piece of paper, try to think not only of its color but also of its tactile qualities, that is, whether you would rather have its surface smooth or rough, fine-grained or coarse-grained. Also think about smell, because paper is often perfumed, especially if it is made by hand or with vegetable fibers.

Deciding on the paper's thickness is the most important step of the whole process. Paper weight is measured in grams per square meter (gsm). Start with mass-produced, stiff, compact cards weighing 140–160 gsm. As they are not very thick, these cut well, their fiber is easily identifiable (see page 16), and they allow for a precise and lasting fold. Remember that if excessively lightweight material is used, the model will not stand up under its own weight, nor will it bend or fold properly. If, on the other hand, the card is too heavy, obtaining the perfect fold and closure will prove difficult.

A wide range of paper and cards are available from stationers, paint shops, or graphic design shops. Buy some good-quality industrial paper to start with and only later go for the more expensive papers, which are more difficult to cut and fold. Avoid using acid containing papers in order to ensure that your models last without fading or yellowing.

To preserve paper well, whatever type it may be, remember that it is necessary to store it away from the sun, in a dry place and on a flat surface, rolling it up only for short periods of time.

Below is an outline of the various types of paper and cards that are available on the market.

WHITE CARDS

White paper possesses numerous expressive possibilities, especially if one exploits its plays of light and shade. Furthermore, it can be used for both trial runs and finished objects. If you are not too familiar with colors, a piece of white paper will always give a good result. The types of white paper most suitable for the models depicted in this manual weigh between 160 and 200 gsm and

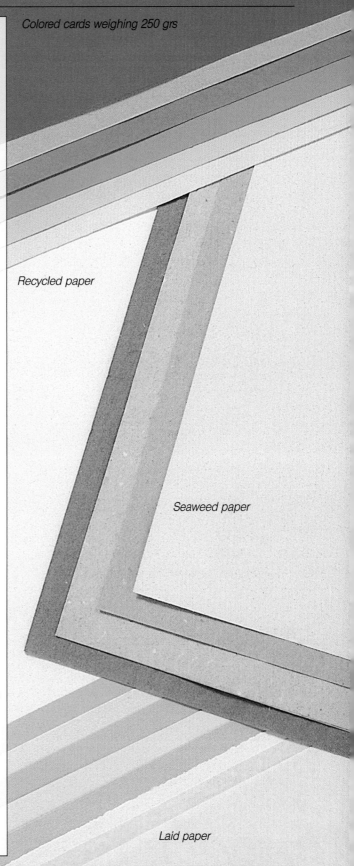

Colored cards weighing 250 grs

have either smooth or rough surfaces. For the less complex models, it is also possible to use the coarse-grained, stiff, or soft cards normally used for watercolor drawings; or cotton cards, which are very soft.

COLORED CARDS

These are the most widely used in this manual. Some, produced in Italy and France and weighing 160 gsm, have both a smooth and a rough surface. By exploiting this difference, you will obtain expressive results. This type of paper benefits by being compact, acid-free and by having an alcaline reserve — characteristics which guarantee that color will not fade with time.
A wide variety of colored cards are available on the market. Choose those with a maximum thickness of 250 gsm. Most important is that the paper be colored directly in the pulp and not on the surface. In the latter case, in fact, folds or cuts are likely to expose the paper's white backing, perhaps ruining the overall effect you were aiming to achieve.

Recycled paper

RECYCLED CARDS

Recycled paper is not especially easy to use, as it is made from a mix of different materials. As a result, while cutting or folding recycled paper, one often encounters various difficulties (lumps, threads, etc.) in the worst places. Make sure you study the paper carefully before purchasing it; observe the number and type of imperfections that characterize it.

SEAWEED PAPER

An Italian paper mill that is particularly aware of environmental issues has been producing this paper for the past two years, obtaining it largely from the excess algae proliferating in the Adriatic Sea. While containing a high percentage of recycled fibers, this paper also boasts excellent workability. It is also endowed with a unique characteristic: with the passing of time, the algae begin to lose chlorophyll and the surface fades, thus becoming increasingly "valuable." It is possible to obtain other kinds of interesting paper, besides seaweed paper, such as that which uses fibers from yearly renewable plants rather than wood paste.

Seaweed paper

LAID PAPER

Laid paper is characterized by a series of parallel lines that can be easily detected on its surface, and that become all the more evident when the sheet of paper is back-lit. The design formed by these lines can be interesting, especially when you are making abstract models.

Laid paper

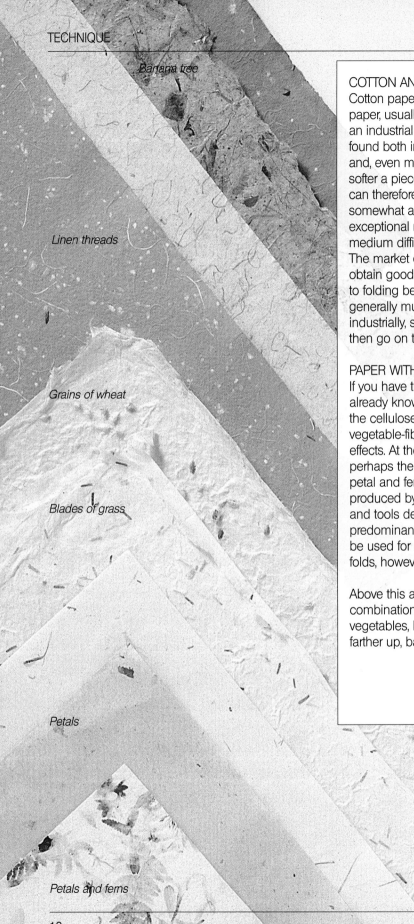

Banana tree

Linen threads

Grains of wheat

Blades of grass

Petals

Petals and ferns

COTTON AND HANDMADE PAPER

Cotton paper is a soft material, unlike woodûfiber paper, usually stiff and compact, and is produced on an industrial scale. This characteristic softness is to be found both in papers produced by industrial machines and, even more so, in those created by hand. The softer a piece of cardboard, the less it holds folds. It can therefore be used only by those who are already somewhat adept and, except in the case of exceptional manual ability, only for models of slight or medium difficulty. But the result is worth that extra effort. The market offers a considerable variety. Be sure to obtain good-quality paper and observe how it reacts to folding before starting your work. Quality paper is generally much more expensive than paper produced industrially, so try out the cheaper material first and then go on to smaller-sized sheets.

PAPER WITH VEGETABLE FIBERS

If you have tried to make paper yourself, you will already know that any type of fiber may be added to the cellulose. This is why there are so many kinds of vegetable-fiber-inlaid paper, with such extremely varied effects. At the bottom of this page we can see what is perhaps the loveliest of these papers — one with petal and fern inserts. The sample shown here was produced by a French paper mill that uses methods and tools derived from the medieval tradition. As it is predominantly made of cotton, it is soft and can even be used for complicated models, which have few folds, however.

Above this are some examples of possible combination of materials — with petals, small vegetables, blades of grass, grains of wheat and, farther up, banana leaves. These examples represent

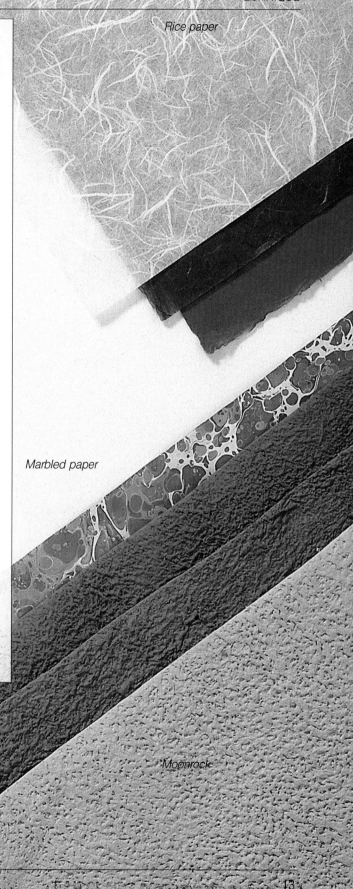

Rice paper

a crescendo in difficulty, owing to the increase in size and in insert-numbers. They make excellent papers for adding luster to a simple design, or for creating a special background. Avoid using them, however, wherever lots of folds or accurate cuts are required. Paper with linen threads and white dots is much easier to handle. As it is cotton-based, it holds folds less well than stiff paper but, if of good quality, gives good results even with complex designs. .

RICE PAPER

This paper is much used in the East. Although very fine, it is quite strong and is therefore suitable for various purposes. Due to its lightness and softness, it is not suitable for making models, but it makes an excellent backing as it allows light to filter through and create special color effects. Be careful, however, when working with glue: it must be used sparingly, spread well, and left to dry to avoid strains forming on the paper's surface.

MOONROCK PAPER

This too is a special sort of paper. It is made by small production units in villages in rural India using cotton snippets, and is exported all over the world. Its weight ranges from 160 to 200 gsm. A particular system of production makes it similar to sheet-like paper pulp which, after being damped, can be used for modeling. When used dry, this is an extremely striking paper it must, however, be used with care.

Marbled paper

MARBLED PAPER

Because this paper is usually made with fairly light leaves and strongly marked decorations, whether machine or hand-made, it can only be used as a background.

Moonrock

TOOLS

The projects presented in this manual do not require any particular manual skills, nor any great financial outlay. We do, however, advise that you purchase a cutter, a line-folder, a metal ruler, and a cutting board — all available from stationers and graphic design shops. Only the minimum space is required — a table, even a small one, and a chair in a well-lit position are more than enough. Particular attention must be given to the cutter, which must always be kept sharp but handled with care, and absolutley never left within the reach of small children.

The following pages describe all that is needed to carry out and decorate these projects.

CUTTING AND FOLDING

PENCIL – Use a hard-pointed pencil (H) to trace the pattern and a soft-pointed one (2B) to run over the lines on the back of the pattern to be traced. Alternatively, you can use graph paper, which can be erased like penciling.

ERASER – Used to erase pencil or graph-paper marks left on the paper.

COMPASS – The point of the compass is used to mark the starting and finishing points of the folds and straight lines. It may be substituted by a fine metal point or by a large-headed pin.

SET SQUARE AND RULER – These instruments are used to transfer the design onto the sheet of paper and to cut straight lines. At least one of these instruments must be metal, to avoid being damaged by the cutting blade.

CUTTING BOARD – This is a rectangle of rather expensive synthetic material, but is a must in order to protect your workplace surface. A piece of thick cardboard may be used instead; it is cheaper but less long-lasting, however,and also rather awkward to use more than once.

CUTTER – Needed to cut the paper. It may be replaced by a scalpel where curved lines are to be cut. The blade can be adjusted in length and slides back completely into the cutter handle; made up of segments, when the blade tip goes blunt, you only

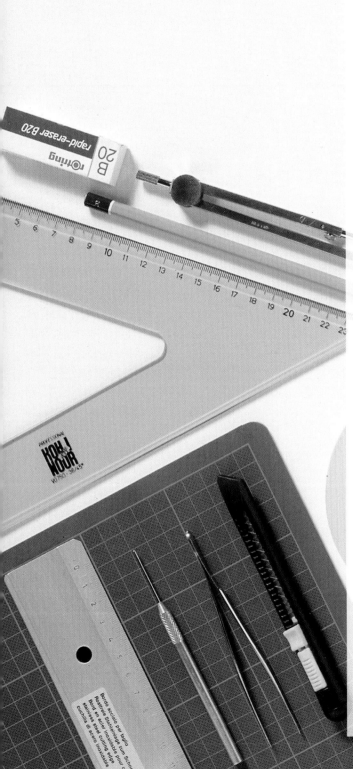

need to break off the top segment. A sharp blade is thus always available.

LINE FOLDER – This is a metal instrument with a fine, rounded point that creases folds. It is on sale from the better graphic suppliers. A fine hook or an empty ball-point pen may be used instead, but with less satisfactory results.

TWEEZERS – These help to fold small parts or parts that are hard to get at with fingers in the more complex models.

PAPER ADHESIVE – This is mainly used to secure the drawing to the paper. It is a light tape that can be placed in position various times.

TRANSPARENT TAPE – Some rare use is made of this on the back of the paper to correct cutting mistakes.

GLUE – This is used to stick on the backing sheet where required. It is advisable to use a vinyl-free, glue to reduce the risk of the paper warping.

DECORATING

PENCILS AND FELT PENS – These are used to add color, particularly to child-oriented models.

INDIA INK – This represents the basic element for Suminagashi, the technique of decorating paper to resemble marbling. Black, blue, and red are the traditional colors, but all shades may be used. A basin of water and kitchen paper are also required for this technique.

ESSENCE OF TURPENTINE – This is used as an alternative to India ink to create the Suminagashi effect.

PAINTBRUSHES AND DIPPING CUPS – These are used to dilute or mix colors for wash drawings, watercolors, and Suminagashi. They must be cleaned thoroughly after each use.

TOOTHBRUSH – This is used to spray color over small-sized cards. This is a quick way out for those of you who can't use, or are not a dab hand at using, a spray gun.

TEMPERA COLORS – We recommend you only buy the basic colors (yellow, magenta and cyan, black, and white) and mix them together to make the other colors needed for the spraying technique.

WATERCOLORS – These are particularly suitable for achieving soft-hued decorations. Be careful not to use too much water, otherwise the card will bend under its own weight.

BASIC TECHNIQUES

Technique is the key to achieving good results; it serves to increase one's know-how and skills, and opens the path to creativity. Read these pages carefully and don't hesitate to look things up, should you want to refresh your memory regarding certain steps. It is not important that you learn everything immediately; it is sufficient to remember the basic techniques. If you can't remember something, you can always look it up. If while reading this manual you should find something unclear, try making the example depicted on that particular page: direct experience is very often an eye-opener.

DETERMINING THE GRAIN

The fibers in factory-made paper follow a precise direction, one parallel to one of the sides of the sheet of paper and one equivalent to the direction of the conveyor belt that takes the paper from the humid to the dry area in production machinery.
The fibers in handmade paper, on the other hand, are randomly arranged and it is therefore impossible

to identify their exact direction. Determining the grain direction in a card allows you to exploit its properties to the utmost, and consequently makes it possible to obtain an easy, accurate, and long-lasting fold.
When making models, be sure to exploit this characteristic to your advantage. When using light paper, transfer the drawing onto the card in such a way as to have the folding lines perpendicular to the grain direction. This will allow you to enhance the piece of paper's stiffness and obtain a more long-lasting fold.
If, on the contrary, you are using a heavier card, make sure that the folds are parallel to the grain direction. In this way, all folding operations will become easier, and irregular or jagged borders along the folds will be avoided.
To understand this second point better, study the photo on the right in which are depicted two folding lines made on thick cards. The more perfect fold was made by folding the card along the grain direction, while the wrinkled one was made by folding the paper with the grain perpendicular to the fold.

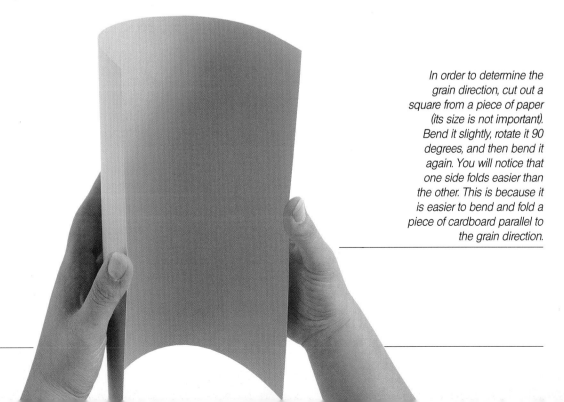

In order to determine the grain direction, cut out a square from a piece of paper (its size is not important). Bend it slightly, rotate it 90 degrees, and then bend it again. You will notice that one side folds easier than the other. This is because it is easier to bend and fold a piece of cardboard parallel to the grain direction.

MOUNTAIN AND VALLEY FOLDS

Mountain and valley folds play an extremely important role in this paper craft as they are the basis for all models. A few cuts and folds are all it takes to turn a two-dimensional sheet of paper into a three-dimensional object. Take a piece of paper and fold it in half. A mountain fold is when the external part of a folded piece of paper is visible, like the lavender-colored card in the photograph. Seen from the side, a piece of paper folded with a mountain fold is like an upside-down V. Now turn the paper over. What you have in front of you is a valley fold similar to the green piece of cardboard in the photograph. A valley fold is therefore a mountain fold seen from the back and vice versa. The definition of mountain and valley is therefore always relative to the point of observation. Cuts and mountain and valley folds are represented by precise symbols in drawings, similar to those used in origami.

In the diagrams depicted, the cutting line will be represented by a continuous straight line, the mountain fold by a dotted line, and the valley fold by a dashed line. In this manual, you will also find a set of symbols referring to the level of difficulty of the cutting and folding procedures needed to make the models. One asterisk means that the project is easy, two mean it is of medium difficulty, and three that the model is complex.

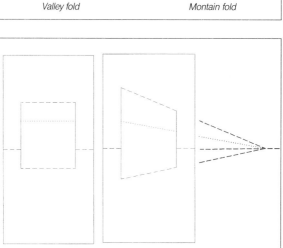

Valley fold   *Montain fold*

SOME PRACTICE

To become acquainted with the mountain and valley folding system, try out the two examples depicted on this page. Take a rectangular card and draw a line down the middle of its long side. This is the central valley fold. Now draw two lines perpendicular and asymmetrical to the central line, and cut them. Join the two ends of the cut sections with two valley lines parallel to the central fold.

In order for a parallelepiped shape to surface from the piece of paper, it is necessary to make a mountain fold. This must be as far from the valley line farthest from the middle of the piece of paper as the closest line is far from the central valley. Fold the piece of paper thus drawn and you will have made a model according to the valley-mountain folding technique.

Folds can also be oblique. In this case, the folding lines must all converge at a point pertaining to the central valley, as shown in the second diagram.

Moreover, the corner in the middle between the closest valley and the central one must measure the same as that between the farthest valley and the mountain fold. In this way you will have obtained a basic converging and folding model.

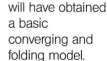

CREASING AND SCORING

There are a variety of methods which make folding operations easier. The most common are the continuous or dashed scoring technique and the creasing technique.

Never carry out these operations directly on your working surface as it could be damaged. If possible, place a cutting board underneath the sheet of paper.

SCORING – It consists in cutting the side of the mountain fold with the tip of the cutter. The cut should be as deep as half the thickness of the paper used. This helps make sharp, neat cuts, but on the other hand weakens the paper.

Scoring is absolutely necessary when using thick pieces of card and paper, but may be replaced by the creasing technique when finer or handmade papers are used.

DASHED SCORING – It is achieved following the same principles as the above instruction. In this case, however, the cut is not unbroken, but is interrupted at regular intervals. This allows you to determine the degree of pliability that may be given to the piece of paper, in accordance with the ratio between the cuts and the uncut segments. The longer the cuts, the greater the flexibility of the card and vice versa. Compared to the scoring technique, this method guarantees greater paper resistance, but is more difficult to do.

In the CREASING technique, pressure is applied to a card's folding line with a rounded metallic point.
To carry out this operation the following can be used: a line folder, a bone folder, a fine hook, or an ink-free ballpoint pen. Creasing is always done along the valley part of the fold.

This technique does not weaken the sheet of paper and guarantees a neat fold when used with lightweight cards. It is also ideal for soft papers such as those containing a high percentage of cotton, but it is less suited to thicker pieces of paper.

A TYPOLOGY OF FOLDS

90°

This is the most commonly used type of fold; it illustrates the change from two-dimensional sheets of paper to three-dimensional models particularly well. A piece of card that has been drawn on and scored becomes three-dimensional at 90 degrees, and once again two-dimensional at 180°. To make this model, at least two valley folds and one mountain fold are needed, besides the central valley one. Depicted on this page is a technique that also requires the so-called sectioning that frees a part of the mountain and valley folds. This gives the shape a greater liveliness, as the parts thus sectioned may be lifted out of, or folded into, the original parallelepiped form.

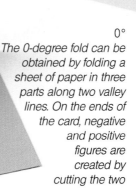

0°

The 0-degree fold can be obtained by folding a sheet of paper in three parts along two valley lines. On the ends of the card, negative and positive figures are created by cutting the two borders together or separately. In the first case, it is necessary to slip a card between the areas to be cut and the part that will serve as backing sheet, i.e., the area in between the card, so as to prevent it from being cut with the cutter.

TUNNEL

The tunnel fold makes it possible to create miniature stage sets, in which the perspective effect is particularly evident. Contrary to the other types of fold, the central fold is a mountain and not a valley one. The drawing always develops on different levels, starting from the two levels pertaining to the simplest project.

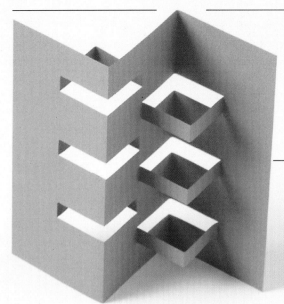

0°

The foundation paper for this type has a mountain and a valley fold that can divide the surface into equal or different parts. In order to make shapes rise from the sheet of paper, it is possible to use both lines – as is the case in the example depicted on the left – or only one line. Each one of the two folds, for example, can be considered as the central line of a 90-degree model.

180°

Contrary to the 90°degree type, this model takes on its final shape only if it is opened to 180 degrees. The sheet of paper resembles a W, with its lateral sides leaning against the surface. At least two lateral valley folds and one central mountain fold are necessary to obtain this structure. Usually these 180-degree models need a backing sheet so that they can be opened and closed time and time again.

180° SLOTTED MODEL

Unlike the previous 180-degree model, the structure for this fold does not require a backing sheet. The whole drawing is obtained from a single sheet of paper and the shapes are kept in place thanks to one or more simple slots, as depicted in the example on the left. The main fold is achieved by a central valley fold and another two valley creases at the foot of the shapes that are to be slotted.

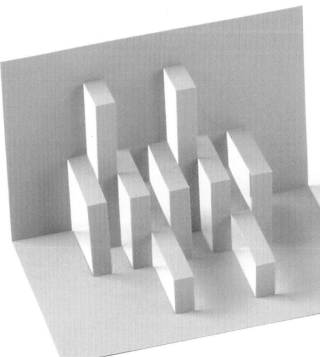

PARALLEL FOLDS
Most of the models depicted in this manual use valley and mountain folds parallel to the central line. The same bases described on the two previous pages were all made with a parallel folding system. Once folded, the parts of the drawing that develop according to this technique emerge from the foundation sheet of paper in a perfectly perpendicular manner. Turn back to the simple example given on page 18, if the valley-mountain-valley folding system is unclear to you, or try copying the models on pages 20 and 21. The latter will be good practice.

CONVERGING FOLDS
As already seen in the previous chapter, the set of folds that create a model can also be converging. If in fact you would like to use oblique folding lines, they must meet at a point relating to the central line, be it mountain or valley. The folding system for oblique lines allows the parts of the model to move, almost as if they were bowing, towards this converging point. If the subject is made up of many disconnected parts, each one turns to a different meeting point, thus forming a shape similar to an opening and closing mouth.

GENERATIONS

Every generation begins from the basic valley-mountain-valley system. From a simple or complex solid made with two cuts and three folds, it is possible to obtain a series of other ever-smaller solids. All you need to do is use each lateral valley fold of the first generation as if it were the central fold for the creation of a new solid, which thus becomes the second generation. In order to do this, you can use both sides, or only one, according to the effects you would like to achieve. Generations are usually symmetrical to the central valley folds, but can also be asymmetrical.

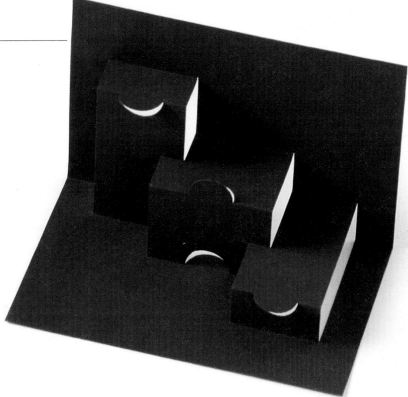

MULTI-LEVEL MODELS

A 90- or 180-degree model can be made from a single solid with varying degrees of complexity, or from a multi-piece set. This second example requires a multi-level project. In the simplest examples, each level is connected to the bottom but is disconnected from the rest of the levels. In the more complex ones, instead, everything is strictly linked. Among this group are stairway-type structures. The multi-level system is generally asymmetrical to the central valley, but can also be the result of a combination between symmetry and asymmetry.

WORK PHASES

Having learned all about the basic techniques and become acquainted with the various types of folds that can be made, the moment has come to understand how to obtain a three-dimensional object simply by using a piece of paper and a cutter. Carefully read and try out the examples depicted on the following pages, so as to become familiar with this versatile method, which can be adopted no matter what kind of model you intend to make. Along with the photographs, you will also find the drawings of the models that serve as examples. It is extremely useful to follow the various steps while cutting and folding a sheet of paper or card.

TRASFERRING PATTERNS ONTO A CARD

There are various methods for transferring a pattern onto a card, which then allow it to be folded and cut. Below is a list of possible techniques and an in-depth explanation of the two most commonly used methods:

The most useful method for learning this technique is to re-draw the model completely. The technique may be used for very simple models, but becomes burdensome when making more complex ones. Another technique consists in retracing the pattern by placing the model on a glass surface, illuminated by a source of light. It can be very handy if the right elements are available.

The third technique consists of first re-tracing the model onto acetate. The pattern thus obtained may be used time and time again when transferring the model onto card with the aid of graph paper. Be careful, however, because "double tracing" tends to make the final drawing inaccurate.

The following are the two most commonly used techniques:

PIERCING (for drawings made with straight lines). Photocopy the drawing, using the scale that you prefer or the one specified in the instructions. Cut a couple of strips of paper adhesive and stick them to

your fingers so that they lose a little of their glue and consequently don't damage the softer cards. Attach

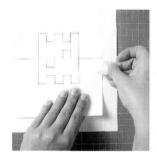

the photocopy to your chosen piece of card with a strip of cellophane tape. Using the point of a compass, pierce the ends of the folding and cutting lines. Be careful not to exert too much pressure when doing this, or you will create a series of visible perforations along the piece of cardboard. When removing the photocopy, you will notice a series of small perforations on the piece of paper. These serve to mark the folds and to cut the models.

TRACING (for patterns made of curved and mixed lines). If the pattern presents curved lines, the method described above is not suitable, as it would hinder you from understanding the direction of the curve. Slip a piece of tracing paper in between the photocopy and the project card. This allows you to trace the pattern in all its details. Should you not have any tracing paper handy, try coloring the back of the photocopy with a soft-pointed pencil. Whether you

use tracing paper or a pencil, the marks that remain on the card can be easily erased.

MARKING FOLDS

MARKING FOLDS

Marking folds on a card means gently cutting or pressing the folds, so as to make all folding operations easier. When folds are incised, they are called score folds; when they are pressed, they are known as crease folds.

Always mark your folds before cutting, because cutting erases the small holes on the ends of the folding lines. In the chapter on basic techniques, we have already dealt with the two possible folding techniques and explained why it is better to choose one rather than the other. Below, on the other hand, is an explanation of how to make folds starting from the pattern itself. Follow the instructions, and practice by making the two examples proposed here.

Folds are always straight lines and must be made with great care: always use a metal ruler to accompany the cutter or the line folder when scoring or creasing folds.

SCORING

This technique is particularly useful for thick, compact cards and is suitable for those drawings that require precision, such as those in the "Abstract" or

"Architecture" category. Remove the photocopy used for piercing the card. Using a cutter and a ruler, make a slight cut on the mountain part of the fold, halfway through the piece of card, joining the dots marking either end of the line. If this is the first time you're experimenting with this technique, try not to exert too much pressure, or you will cut straight through the card.

Once you have completed the mountain fold, turn the piece of paper over and repeat this operation on the back for those folds that, on the front, are valley folds. You already know that a valley fold is a mountain fold if seen from the back.

CREASING

The creasing technique consists in compressing the folding lines in such a way as to render the card

sufficiently pliable to bend easily. This technique is particularly suitable for those who have no experience in handling a cutter: any mistakes made can be easily corrected. Moreover, the creasing technique is also suitable when using soft, non-homogeneous or light papers.

Remove the photocopy and the tracing paper, if used, from the card. Using a line folder, a hook, or an ink-free ballpoint pen, compress the valley part of the fold. Make sure that the point of the object you are using is rounded, otherwise you risk scratching the sheet of paper and, consequently, of damaging it. Also in this case, join the previously piered ends with the compass and repeat the operation on the back of the card.

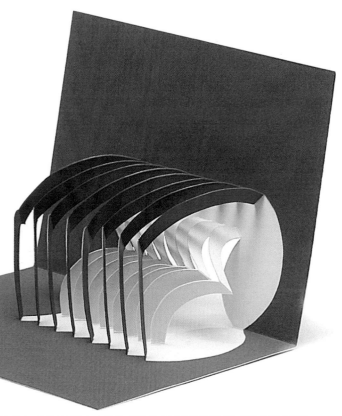

CUTTING

In order to obtain an accurate, clean cut relatively easily, use a sharp, clean cutter or a scalpel blade. Never work directly on a table, but use a cutting board. Using newspaper or cardboard for this purpose is not ideal, for they tend to tear easily. Furthermore, the cutter may well follow the direction of the newspaper instead of the pattern of the model you are making. Cutting boards are certainly more expensive, but the result is excellent, even when they are used repeatedly.

Avoid cutting more than one model at a time because only the first level will come out well. You will have only exerted more pressure to little or no end. When starting to cut – whether in a straight line or a curve – begin with the innermost and smallest lines. On pages 35 and 36, you will find some special tips for cutting small-sized curves or sharp edges. If you follow the two examples given in the previous pages, you will discover two different types of patterns for cutting. One is formed by straight lines and the other comprises both straight lines and curves, or else just curves.

CUTTING STRAIGHT LINES

Straight lines are certainly the easiest to cut. Take a ruler, if possible a metal one, so that it will not be damaged if the cutter blade skids along its surface. Hold the ruler firmly in place and join the holes at both ends of the cutting lines. Should the pattern be

formed by straight and curved lines, cut the traced lines after having cut the curved ones, rather than joining the holes. The longer the line, the greater the difficulty in holding the metal ruler steady.

CUTTING CURVED LINES

When cutting curved lines, it is a good idea to use a scalpel rather than a cutter, so as to have a sharper

blade and a better tip. This is necessary because, in order to obtain a continuous and uninterrupted curve, you must avoid detaching the blade from the page until the curve is completed. If you find this technique difficult to follow at first, try rotating the card instead of moving the blade.

CONTROLLING THE CUT

At the end of this procedure, check that all the parts of the card are perfectly cut; for example, gently push

the model from behind to make sure that there are no corners that do not detach completely from the backing sheet. Should the pattern contain very small elements, check the accuracy of the cut by raising them with the tip of the cutter. Then erase any remaining pencil marks left on the card.

FOLDING

Having checked that the entire model is well cut, you may begin folding. All the models presented here are based on a system of alternating mountain and valley folds. The movements and the procedures to be followed will, however, differ in accordance with the type of model you wish to fold.

For all models, however, we recommend you fold step-by-step. This will avoid forcing the card too much and creating unwanted folds in parts of the model that should remain flat. In other words, you should first slightly bend the mountain and valley folds of the whole model and then fold them more and more, until they reach their final position. At this point, you can press the sheet of paper and open it again to make sure that the opening and closing movements function properly.

SYMMETRICAL 90°DEGREE MODELS

Models made symmetrically at 90° to the central folding line are among the easiest to fold. Usually,

they are based on a "one mountain and two valley folds" system that allows them to meet at the central valley fold. This base can be enriched with a series of concentric patterns; these help create attractive effects such as those for the star or the heart. To fold this type of model, begin by bending the piece of card slightly so that the

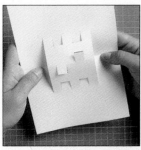

parallelepiped that makes up the end result stand out from the backing sheet.

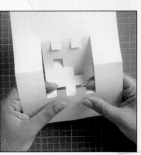

Now make valley folds of the central and two side lines. To do this easily, turn the card over and press the mountain part of the folds as indicated in the photograph. On the face of the card, make the mountain fold that will highlight the three-dimensional form of the model. Be careful not to bend the little squares that have been obtained

through sectioning. Now fold the whole model and flatten it. Re-open and check that it functions properly and that there are no defects. It is worth mentioning the zero model in particular. This type can be classified

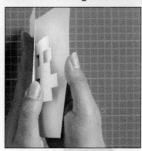

either as falling into the 90°degree symmetrical or asymmetrical kind, depending on how these models are patterned. This is because the zero structure can be divided into various parts, each of which will gravitate around a fold and can in every way be considered a 90° degree model.

90-DEGREE MULTI-LEVEL MODELS

Ninety-degree multi-level systems are the most used

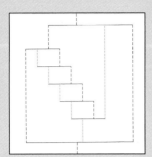

in making models, because of their very attractive possibilities. With a multi-level, we can construct increasingly difficult projects, formed by full and empty volumes, stairways, geometric solids, or indefinite shapes. Such shapes are generally asymmetric with regard to the central fold. The starting point in carrying out the fold is more or less the same as the symmetrical type with regard to the central fold. In fact, this and the previous model have both 90° folds. Later, however, multi-level projects differ and reveal their folding complexity.

The example proposed here is characterized by a composition between an asymmetric parallelepiped with regard to the central valley, and a stairway.

Having checked the cut and erased any pencil marks, begin folding as already shown for the symmetrical model; that is, bend the model slightly forward, along the central valley fold. Contrary to the previous model, this will not stand out easily from the card and will need further manipulation.

Now turn the piece of cardboard over and exert some pressure on the central fold, on the basic fold, and on that which distances the parallelepiped from the backing sheet. It is often easier to make a mountain fold than a valley one, and for this reason we often advise making some folds while observing the back of the sheet of paper. Facing once more the front of the

sheet, gradually fold the mountain line that defines the parallelepiped and those of the five steps. In order to fold the stairway, place your fingers between it and the rest of the foundation paper. This will help you to put pressure on the folds and obtain the final result more easily.

If you have marked the valley and mountain lines well, you will be able to fold the whole model without forcing the piece of cardboard too much. The result will be perfect, with clear folds on flat surfaces that are neither damaged nor bent.

GENERATIONS

A parallelepiped obtained from the valley fold of a 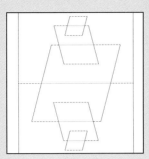 card generates to two new valley folds. These can be used to create new shapes for which the foundation card consists of the wall of the parallelepiped and the base of the original piece of cardboard. The new shapes thus obtained can also give rise to new cuts and folds. This system can be developed endlessly. The structures, which reveal their nature during the act of folding, are known as generations. In the more simple examples, the folds that constitute generations are parallel to each other and the shapes are symmetrical to their reference valley fold. The more complex cases, instead, can consist in converging folds and asymmetrical structures. The example proposed on this page is one of the simplest, and helps clarify the generation-making mechanism.

Begin by folding the first parallelepiped-shaped form  like a symmetric 90°. Fold the central valley, the central mountain fold and, only slightly, the lateral valleys. A structure of this kind can be made with relatively lightweight pieces of cardboard, as every step of the folding procedure further stiffens the model.

Use the two lateral valleys as base folds to make other solids. Every time you have to make a new  generation, imagine you're starting from scratch. In this way you will obtain a central valley (the one considered lateral in the previous generation), two central valleys, and a mountain valley. As you fold this part, the rest of the model remains unchanged. Repeat this same procedure for the other side of the model.

By making generation after generation, the final shape is obtained. Always remember to fold

 completely, to flatten, and to open the model so as to verify whether the folds are in the right places and the movements are as desired.

TUNNEL

The basic premise of the tunnel fold is completely

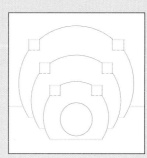

different from that of the previous models. Upon closer observation, it is really a 90-degree model with, however, a central mountain folding line instead of a central valley fold. Besides this, the model develops on ever-more different levels, thus creating an attractive perspective effect, very similar to a stage set. With the tunnel model, every level is connected to both the previous and the next ones through "spacers," formed by two pieces of paper folded with a mountain and a valley fold. Look carefully at the pictures and copy the hand movements in folding the tunnel and the spacers.

stiff, but not heavy, kind of paper is highly recommended. The example proposed on this page, like those on the previous pages, was made with a piece of resistant compact card weighing 160 gsm, well suited for the kind of movements the tunnel model requires of the paper. Once again remember that, contrary to the models presented on the previous pages, the tunnel's central mountain fold faces the observer.

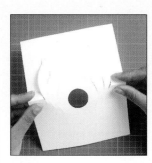

Cut and remove the circle at the center of the model. Erase any pencil marks left on the sheet of paper. Now begin to fold the model from the central mountain fold. Pinch the mountain lines, at the foot of each level, into folds. This series of mountain folds defines the depth of the project's perspectival field.

When making this type of model, it is especially

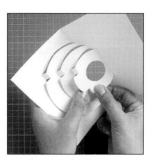

important to fold gradually so as to prevent the spacers from folding badly and consequently losing their perspectival effect. Follow, as already mentioned, the movements of the hands depicted in the photographs, and pull one level onto the other so as to create mountain and valley folds ù as depicted in the photos.

The structure will gradually acquire its three-dimensional shape and you will be able to fold it back on itself a bit at a time. To make this model a

180°

As you probably know by now, there are various 180-

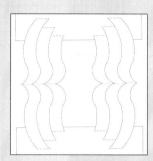

degree that can be divided into two major categories: the simple ones and the slotted ones. The diagram on the left pertains to the first and more complex of these groups, while for the second group a few brief explanations will suffice.

The folding system for a 180-degree slit-and-slot model is decidedly very simple. It consists of one central valley fold and two valley folds, both at the base of the parts that need to be slotted or glued (very rare). The two lateral folds therefore lift the subject from the sheet of paper from which it originates. Once the two parts have been lifted, they must be slotted in accordance with the instructions described in the pictures.

When, instead, a simple 180-degree model is needed, the folding system takes on an important role and serves to raise the whole motif from the surface. Furthermore, a support for the folds is necessary, and this can be obtained with a backing sheet that holds the model's two outermost sides

together. To fold the piece of paper, start from the mountain valley at the center of the pattern. In the example depicted on the left, the subject is made up of various curved segments, which means, therefore, that there will be as many

mountain folds as there are elements in the patterns. The mountain valley draws the two outer sides closer,

and these must subsequently remain closed.

Now fold the valley folds at the base of each of the elements. This operation must be repeated for both sides of the model. In this way every one of the segments, which are similar to

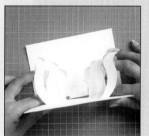

curly brackets, will acquire a different height and opening.

To complete the model, close the two external sides of the card so as to form a surface. Stick them together temporarily with two strips of paper tape and open and close the model several times to check that it works well. To finish off, replace the provisional hook with a sheet of backing paper. To do this, follow the instructions set out on the following page.

APPLYNG A BACKING SHEET

Apart from the 180-degree type model, the projects in the next sections of this manual do not need a support to open and close correctly. The choice of using a backing sheet therefore need not be dictated by necessity, but simply by the desire to make a model more interesting. In the 180-degree, W-type models, the backing paper instead is used to draw the two outermost sides of the structure closer to fix the shape in the right position. The procedure for inserting the backing sheet is, however, the same for both the 90-degree and 180-degree models. Should the model be a 180-degree slotted one, remember to cut the backing sheet in half before gluing it. Depicted here are two examples that can be made easily. The first uses a gluing method that renders the foundation and backing sheet more solid. The second exploits a slotting system between two sheets of paper, which makes it possible for the foundation sheet to be released from, and reinserted into, the backing paper time and again.

THE GLUING METHOD

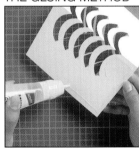

Once the model has been folded, cut out a rectangle the same size or slightly bigger than the first and fold it in half. Keeping the model folded, spread a little glue on the back of one half. This will prevent you from making mistakes, because it helps you to understand immediately which parts must, and which must not, be glued.

Lay the half that is glued on the backing sheet so that the central folds of the two sheets of paper are adjoining and the model is in place. Press well, starting from the center of the piece of paper outwards. If you find that there is excessive glue along the sides, do not press further, to avoid

staining the cards. Fold the side of the model still free almost completely, spread it with glue, and repeat the above-mentioned operations.

THE SLOTTING METHOD

In this case, the backing sheet must be slightly bigger than the model. After having cut the card, draw on it the outline of the model so that it is centered.

Make the slot cuts on the four corners of the pattern. The simplest type is a 45-degree line that joins two sides at one or more centimeters from the corner. Depicted in the photograph is the "ladder" version.

Check that the cuts are accurate and that the ladder lifts with ease. Insert an edge of the model into one of the slots so that the central folds tally and repeat

this operation for the remaining three edges. To remove the model from the backing sheet, simply pry out the edges of the model from the backing sheet with your finger.

HANDY TIPS

ERASING PENCIL MARKS

Pencil marks remain when we are copying or tracing a model onto a card. Do not use carbon paper instead of tracing paper, otherwise the pattern

remains indelible. Once you have marked the folds with your favorite technique and completed all cutting procedures, gently erase any marks still visible with a clean, white eraser for pencils. Use your other hand to flatten the cut parts and

then run the eraser along the cutting lines. These handy tips help to prevent any involuntary lifting or folding of the edges.

CUTTING SHARP CORNERS

When cutting sharp edges, if too much pressure is exerted and the wrong direction is taken, the tips follow the cutter and wrinkle up. To prevent this from happening and to avoid having the characteristic "X" appear on the sheet of paper due to excessively long cuts, follow the instructions outlined below. Check that the cutter blade is clean and sharp. Begin by cutting the innermost parts of the drawing. When you get to a corner, cut the first side slowly so as to arrive exactly at the corner without going beyond it. Marking the pattern with the point of the compass can be useful as long as the holes are small, otherwise the tips of the model will turn out inaccurately.

To cut the following side, do not start from the tip, but from the opposite end, as indicated in the photograph. In this way the tip will remain fixed to the card to the last, without risk of getting ruined.

RIGHTING A WRONG CUT

If you have cut in the wrong place or prolonged a cut more than necessary, do not throw your piece of paper away. Instead use an invisible tape or secure a small strip of lightweight paper and a little glue on the back of the sheet to close the cut. Always check that the model opens and closes without difficulty. Remember, however, that with time both glue and tape make paper turn yellow.

A STAIN OF GLUE

It often happens that too much glue is used to attach a piece of paper to a backing sheet and that, while pressing, some of it oozes out, staining the paper. If you are using a vinyl-free glue, try to follow these simple instructions. Remove as much glue as possible with the tip of your cutter. Try not to spread it, and be decided in your movements. When only a thin layer of glue is left on the sheet of paper, erase it energetically with an eraser. For this operation to work, the glue must not yet be completely dry. Check frequently on the state of things and take care not to exaggerate for fear of ruining the card. A special kind of eraser is available on the market which is

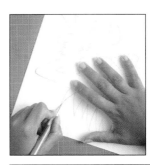

mainly used by graphic designers and which is perfect for erasing any excessive glue. It is used just like a pencil eraser and can be found in the better-stocked graphic design shops

PERFECT CIRCLES

Small circles are the most difficult shapes to cut. Cutting curved lines without ever removing the cutter from the drawing may at times prove difficult. In this case, try out this method: Cut the circle without worrying too much about the edge being too segmented. Try, however, not to go over the same points several times and, above all, take your time. In this way, you will have avoided cutting long

segments at a tangent from the circle. Once you have completed this operation, take a line folder (a propelling pencil or any other object with a round tip will do as long as it has a diameter greater than that of the circle you cut) and a coned point. Check that the object is clean. Slip the tip through the hole of the card until it can go no farther and rotate with determination.
This movement helps to round the segmentation along the edge of the cut

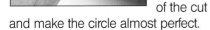

and make the circle almost perfect.

TRIMMING THE EDGES

If you decide to apply a backing sheet to the model, you may use two pieces of paper different or equal in size. In the former case, after having glued the two

cards together, check that their borders are parallel. It can in fact happen, especially if one is working in a rush, that the two sheets of paper move during the gluing phase. Should this be the case, use the cutter and the metal ruler to trim the

outer border so that it becomes parallel to the internal one. This is usually done with the model completely open.
Where the two cards are equal in size, close the model and check whether the internal sheet is visible or not. Press the sheets of paper with the metal ruler and trim the borders with the cutter. If the difference between the two sheets is greater than 5 mm, take care not to cut the subject as well as the border. Open the model and check from the inside to be sure the borders of the backing sheet are not visible. Should this be so, close the model and trim once more.

DECORATING

Most models do not need to be decorated on the surface, but express their charm thanks to the play of light and shadows that is created through the various levels. In Japan these types of model are in fact almost exclusively made with white paper. It may be interesting from time to time, however, to add some color, and this may be done either by selecting colored paper or employing some decorative techniques. The latter must be simple, however, a kind of final touch, and must not be a cause of distraction from the construction of the model with the techniques described until now.

When you decorate a model, make sure to work in an aired room with lots of light. Cover your worksurface top with newspapers before arranging on it the colors, water, and other materials you will need in the course of your work.

TOOLS
Tempera colors
Paintbrush
Dipping cups
Toothbrush
Gloves

SPRAY COLORING

This is one of the simplest and quickest decoration techniques. You need only spray a little color on the model with tempera colors and a toothbrush. Follow the instructions outlined below to learn how to use templates and toothbrushes.

Cut and fold the model. From the photocopy used to

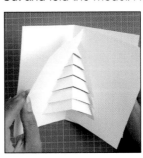

make the project, cut out the shape of the side to be colored. This template is not suitable should you want to decorate the whole card the same color. If, instead, you are interested in using different colors for different areas, prepare one or two templates, cutting out a different part of the drawing in each.

Place the template so as to fit nicely on the folded

card. Secure a couple of strips of adhesive tape to the sides to make perfectly sure that it is fixed well. Dilute the tempera colors until they become soft but

not watery. If you have bought primary colors only, mix them to make the desired color in sufficient quantities. Wear a glove on the hand holding the toothbrush, as it is in direct contact with the colors. Hands soiled by tempera colors are easily washed in water and soap, therefore don't worry if you don't have a pair of gloves handy.

Dip the toothbrush in the color and let it drain a while

before beginning to spray. Press the toothbrush with your index finger; when you let it go, the bristles will spatter color on the sheet of paper. Carry this operation out first on a newspaper, to check that the drops aren't too big. Repeat the procedure a couple of times, moving the model around to decorate its every part in a uniform manner.

Spray one color at a time and clean the toothbrush

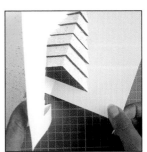

well with water before dipping it into another color. When the model is dry (after ten or fifteen minutes at most), remove the template and check the end result. Should you want to decorate different area with a different color, repeat the said instructions using a new template.

WATERCOLORS

TOOLS

WATERCOLORS
PAINTBRUSH
DIPPING CUPS

Decorating with watercolors requires a bit more experience compared to the previous technique. Don't worry if you've never used these colors: to decorate the models in this book, you need only learn to dose water and colors so as to obtain soft shades of colors. The most interesting feature of watercolors is the luminosity and transparency achieved by diluting the pigments well and endeavoring not to use too much color at a time. This technique moistens the parts of the card to be decorated quite considerably, therefore follow the instructions set out below in order to exploit this to your best advantage.

To obtain good results with watercolors, it is important that the paper used is not too lightweight and that it

absorbs water and pigments well. Therefore, choose the card also according to the decoration you are going to use. Cards specifically designed for watercolors are available on the market; if you are interested in using them, choose the stiffest ones, weighing not more than 220 gsm. Wet the paintbrush well and pass it lightly over the color you intend using. Do not seep it too much in the pigment; in fact, it is best to work step-by-step and go over a color again only if strictly necessary.

If you have used too much color and certain parts of

the model are more colored than others, wet the paintbrush well and pass it over this area so that it absorbs a little of the pigment.

We recommend, however, not to color the whole model, but only certain parts such as the contours or particularly interesting points.

Before the card dries completely, mold it so as to counteract the warping that the water has created in the paper. If you wish the model to be completely flat, place it under weights once it is dry. At times, however, a simple warp can make a model more attractive and more interesting. Therefore, curve the sheet of paper slightly, or some of its parts, thus making the model take on a more attractive roundness.

INDIA INK

This technique is a simplified version of *Suminagashi*, the technique of decorating paper with India inks to resemble the veins of marbled stone, widely used in Japan and China. The traditional colors are blue, black, and red, while the paper most suited for this kind of decoration must be very absorbent and weigh approximately 150 gsm. India ink decorations can be used to color cards which will then be used as backing sheets or as decorative templates for the models. This is because the characteristics needed for decorating with India ink make it unsuitable for folding.

Fill the tray with water. Cut rectangles and squares from the card, about a couple of inches smaller than the size of the tray. Prepare a dipping cup and a paintbrush for every color you intend to use, and an extra one for the turpentine oil. Thin the ink with a drop of turpentine to encourage it to float.

The Orientals use ink in sticks; this is difficult to find in the West.

Dip the clean paintbrush into the turpentine and squeeze it. Remember to close the turpentine flacon, because its exhalations can be harmful. Dip the second paintbrush into the ink with your other hand. Place the two paintbrushes alternately on the water's surface, and a series of concentric circles will form.

When the tray is full of drops of paint, blow softly on the surface to create the vortices of the pattern. Take the card with both hands and lay it carefully on the surface, starting from one end and slowly laying down the rest.

Wait a few seconds, then carefully lift up the paper. The paper will thus absorb the pattern formed by the ink on the water's surface.

Leave the paper to dry horizontally on some kitchen paper or a piece of cardboard. By repeating the same process, but merely changing the colors, the number of circles, or the area in which the paintbrushes touch the surface of the water, it is possible to create papers with very different decorative effects.

IN RELIEF

Besides decorating models with colors, it is also possible to use simple surface treatments that create relief patterns on the sheet of paper. In the following pages you will find three techniques which are among the simplest and quickest to make: piercing, pricking, and bas-relief.

No particular object is needed to carry out these techniques; your basic equipment is sufficient. Some experience and a little imagination are all you need to carry out these techniques in such a way as to highlight the characteristics of the models on which you are experimenting.

PIERCING TECHNIQUE

This technique consists in piercing the card following a precise pattern and creating different-sized holes. The principle is basically the same as that used in the beginning of this section to transfer a pattern onto a card.

Draw a series of holes on the card to form a pattern.

The example on the right depicts a spiral made up of big holes, within which is a series of smaller holes. If the card is not too thick, it is not really necessary to draw directly on it, but with a strip of paper adhesive you can secure a copy of the pattern you wish to carry out for tracing purposes.

With the point of the compass or a very fine graver, make a series of small holes, following the pattern on the card. If you already have an idea of which holes should be larger, put greater pressure according to the width desired. Remember to carry out these operations on a cutting board or a very thick piece of cardboard, so as to avoid ruining your worksurface.

Once this has been completed, erase any pencil marks left on the card and go over the larger holes to make them uniform. The pattern thus obtained will be hollow on the front and in relief at the back.

TOOLS

Pencil
Eraser
Ruler
Compass

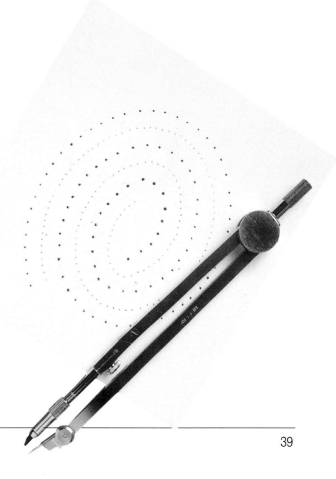

PRICKING TECHNIQUE

With the pricking technique it is possible to achieve a relief drawing made up principally of pricks, but sometimes also of lines, through the use of a line folder. To achieve a good effect, the papers to be used should weigh up to 200 gsm maximum and have a compact, uniform grain.

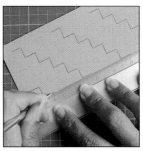

With a pencil, draw the pattern you wish to obtain on the card. Always bear in mind that to achieve the drawing in relief, it will be necessary to prick and then draw on the back of the card. Pass the line folder along the drawing lines and press hard. If you are using a hook or an ink-free ball pen instead of a line folder, don't scratch the card.

Now prick the pattern, pressing the line folder well on each prick. Do not exert too much pressure so as to avoid piercing the paper. Try to make the pricks by keeping the same inclination of the hand and the same pressure, and the end result will as a consequence be more accurate. Now turn over the paper and check the result.

If you find that not all the pricks are visible, press them with the line folder for the second time. The result thus obtained will show up well with a grazing light.

BAS-RELIEF

Bas-relief is a technique that recalls the game children play by putting a coin under a sheet of paper. If the sheet is darkened with a pencil, the underlying pattern comes to the top. Following the same principle, this technique needs a shape in relief placed under the card and pressed until the outlines appear.

As with pricking, to obtain good results a fairly lightweight card is needed (100 gsm is more than enough), compact and stiff like a mass-produced cardboard.

Cut out the figure which you wish to obtain in bas

relief from cardboard at least 3 mm thick. Try to prepare simple shapes, because it will be easier to get them to stand out without slitting or creasing the card.

Secure the shape to the back of the card with cellophane tape. In this way, the bas-relief figure will

have sharp outlines. If, instead, you wish a slight roundness about the figure, secure the shape to the front of the sheet.

Now press lightly with your finger or with the border of a plastic propelling pencil so that the pattern will begin to stand out. Do not press too

hard all at once, because the card could tear. Proceed by successive steps, therefore, until the entire shape comes out in relief.

Remove the tape and the card shape. The outlines of the pattern will remain impressed on the cardboard surface even if you try to flatten it with your hands.

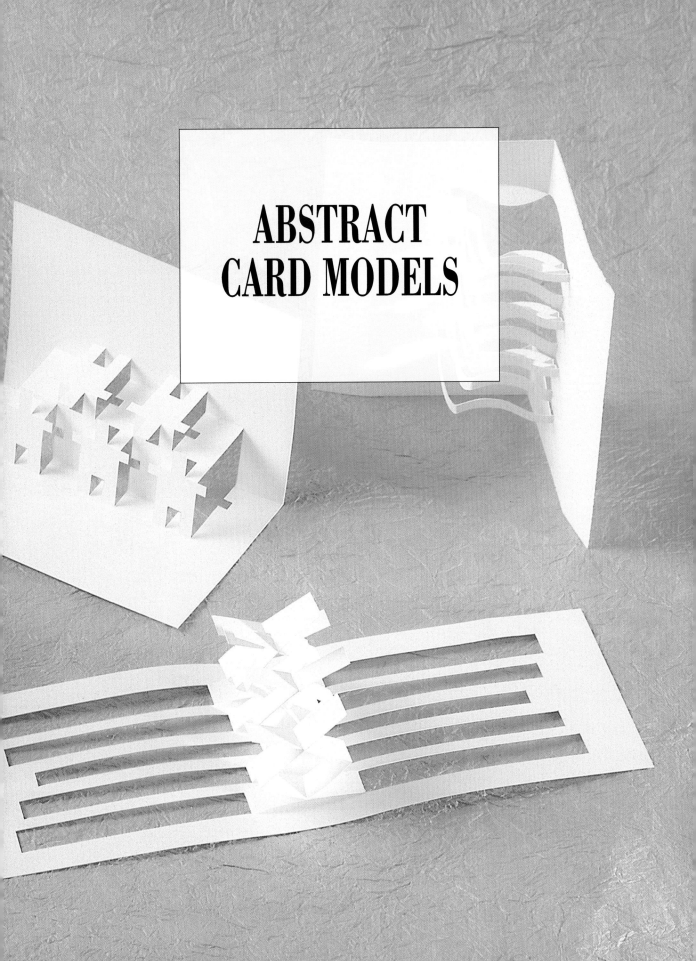

ABSTRACT
CARD MODELS

ZIGZAG

CUTTING DIFFICULTY*
FOLDING DIFFICULTY*
MATERIALS USED: 160 gsm LIGHTWEIGHT GREEN AND BLUE
CARDBOARD
DIMENSIONS: 30 X 10 cm LIGHT GREEN; 31 X 11 cm BLUE

This model has been chosen as a starting exercise. It will help you learn to cut with a cutter and a ruler and to make the basic mountain and valley folds. Try to be very accurate and take your time in following the steps as they are described in these pages. It only takes a little attention to get excellent results.

The pattern made up of straight lines is very simple. The folding is made by a central valley and on each side by a mountain and a valley. It is a 180-degree model enriched by a series of slots. As you can see from the pictures, the whole is derived from just one sheet of light green cardboard, to which a blue background has been added. This is not necessary for the structure but helps to highlight the contrasts between full and empty spaces.

When you have finished the model, try to open it out beyond 180° and then close it various times. The slots will cause the individual strips to rise and fall, as in a dance.

For this, as for most models, movement plays a fundamental part. Kirigami models are almost never static, but reveal their magic when the sheet on which they were created is opened and closed.

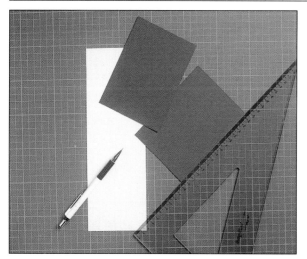

Cut out a 30 x 10 cm rectangle from the light green cardboard and one 31 x 11 cm from the blue. Then cut the blue sheet in half down its length. You will thus have the foundation sheet on which to create the model and the two parts that make up the background.

After having made a 100-percent scale photocopy of the model proposed, secure it to the cardboard with some paper adhesive. To obtain a good result, cut the photocopy to the exact measure or attach the cardboard while holding the pattern against the light.

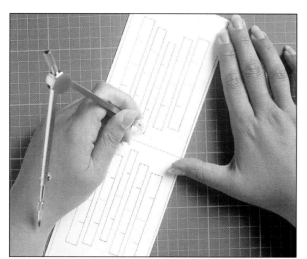

Make small holes at the ends of all the lines on the patterns. Use a compass or some other metal object, for example, a pin, so long as the point is fine enough not to pierce the cardboard too much.

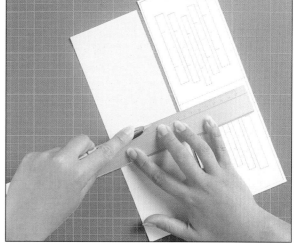

Remove the photocopy from the cardboard, taking care not to damage the sheet. Begin marking the folds, keeping the model beside you to check which lines are to be valley and which mountain. For this operation, follow the instructions on page 25.

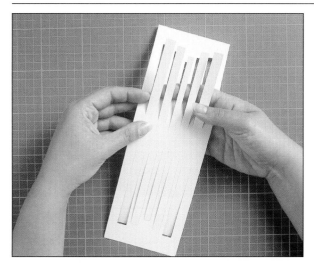

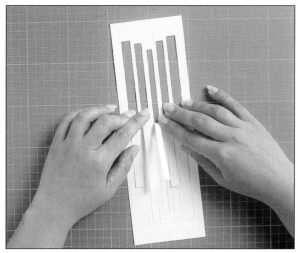

With the cutter, cut the continuous lines in the pattern. All you need to do is join the previously made holes and check the result against the photocopy of the model. By lifting the strips, check that everything has been cut accurately.

Fold and open the cardboard again, along the central valley. Lift the strips and fold them along the valley lines. Having made this movement on one side of the sheet, open the folds again almost completely and repeat the proceedings for the other side.

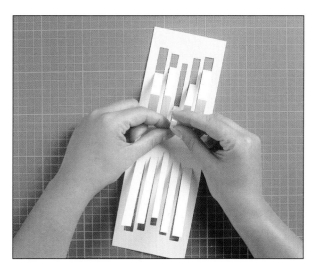

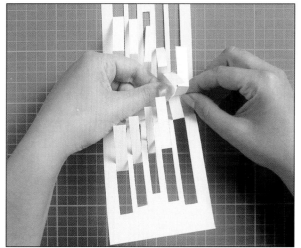

Now fold all the strips one by one mountain-wise, following the hand movements as in the photograph. Press well to obtain a sharp fold and open again lightly. If you have marked the folds well, you won't have any difficulties in carrying out this operation.

The two cuts in each strip serve now for slotting and giving movement to the model. Begin this operation on a side pair and continue towards the opposite side so as not to squash the already slotted strips with your hands.

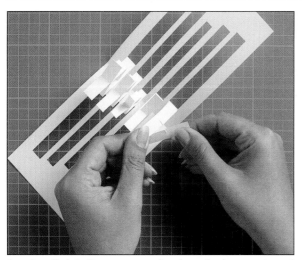
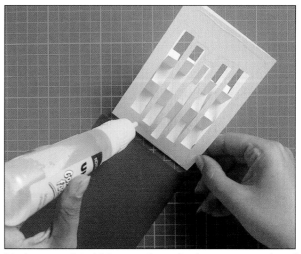

Insert a slip into the one opposite along the lower cuts and then along the higher ones so as to create a double "X." Repeat this operation for the five pairs. You will notice that the structure so formed will be all the higher the nearer the cuts are to the slip bases.

Having completed this operation, take the two rectangles of blue card and the glue. Spread the glue on one half of the green card, keeping the model folded so as not to glue the slips that must be free.

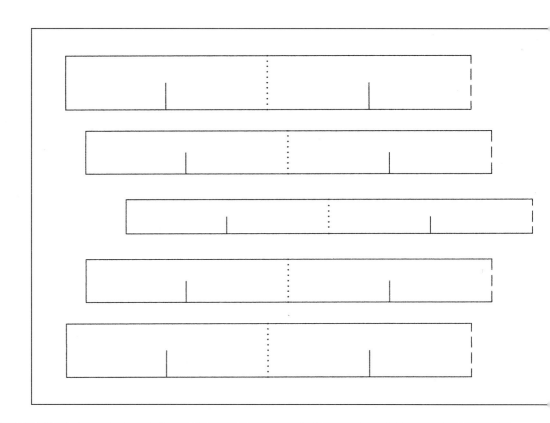

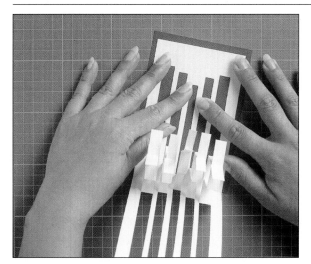

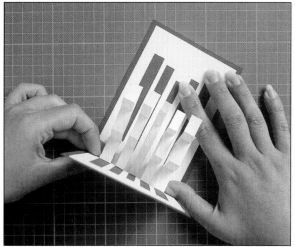

Place the glued part on one of the pieces of blue cardboard, being careful that the fold in the middle of the model coincides with a short side of the blue backing sheet. Check that all the sides of the two sheets are parallel and press hard for a few seconds.

Following the same system, apply the second half of the backing sheet to the model. Between the two blue parts there should be just a small slit. At this point, you need only check that the model works by opening and closing it various times.

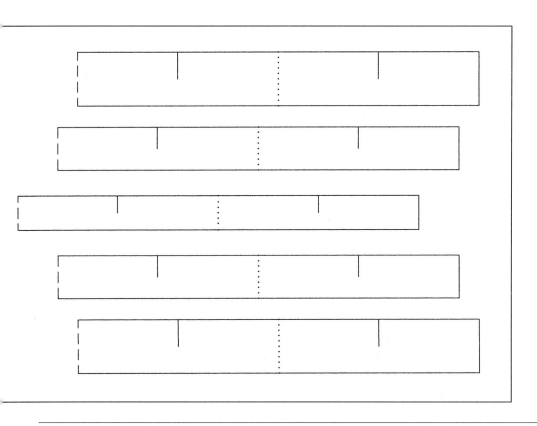

A THREE-FOLD MODEL

CUTTING DIFFICULTY*
FOLDING DIFFICULTY*
MATERIAL USED: 169 gsm LIGHT YELLOW CARDBOARD
DIMENSIONS: 20 X 15 cm
MODEL: PAGE 146
PATTERN TRACING: PAGE 24
CUTTING: PAGE 26
FOLDING: PAGE 28

Here is the first model to try out on your own: it is a classical 90-degree model following the valley-mountain-valley system. The pattern is asymmetrical with respect to the central valley fold. Cutting and folding is here slightly more complex than for the previous model, but it is really just as easy to make. Simply pay particular attention when cutting to avoid tearing the corners of the pattern while folding. If you feel confident in using the cutter, use the scoring system to mark the folds (all mountain-wise). If not, we recommend you crease valley-wise for this model and for those you intend to make in the immediate future. In this way, any errors made will be easily rectified. When folding, start from the longest lines — in this case from the central valley. If you want an accurate result, use the well-sharpened cutter with attention and without haste.

To understand what the final result will be, observe the lateral view well. It will help you to get a clearer idea of how the model must be folded.

It was here decided not to insert a backing sheet. If you want to make a present of this card, you can attach a card, taking care when spreading glue on the model folded at 90°, so as to be sure not to glue the parts that are to remain free.

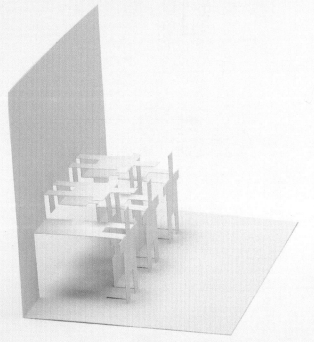

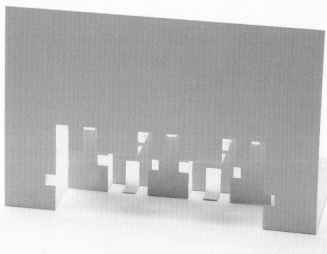

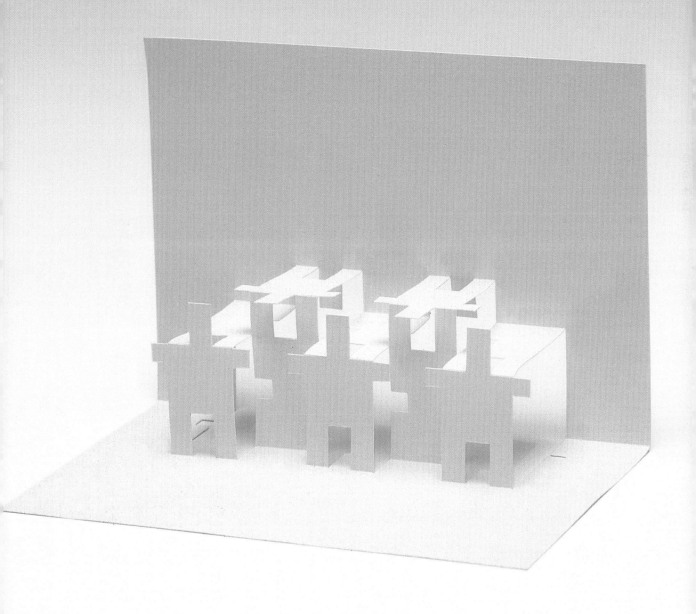

WAVES

CUTTING DIFFICULTY*
FOLDING DIFFICULTY*
MATERIAL USED: 200 gsm SEAWEED PAPER AND 160 gsm GREEN
COTTON PAPER
DIMENSIONS: 20 X 15 cm SEAWEED PAPER; 72 X 17 cm COTTON

MODEL: PAGE 146
TRACING: PAGE 24
CUTTING: PAGE 26
FOLDING: PAGE 27

This project represents a further step ahead: cutting curved lines. You can see from the picture that these lines are not very pronounced and are suitable for gaining confidence in copying and cutting freehand. Again we have the simplest type of 90-degree folding (valley-mountain-valley). You will notice, however, that it takes longer to fold this sheet because you have to accompany each strip in the folding to be sure of a good result. From the pictures, you can see clearly that the folding system is symmetrical with respect to the central axis. A further variation is represented by the application of the backing sheet without the use of glue. You only need a slightly bigger card (1 cm per side) in which to cut the stairs in correspondence with the corners of the sheet of seaweed paper, as marked on the design. The next step is to insert the corners of the foundation sheet into the slots made in the backing cardboard. The project is thus completed.

This system can be used for all those models that call for a backing sheet. It is particularly useful for those who are not especially expert in the use of glue or whenever one wishes to make a present of a card with no backing sheet and without using an envelope.

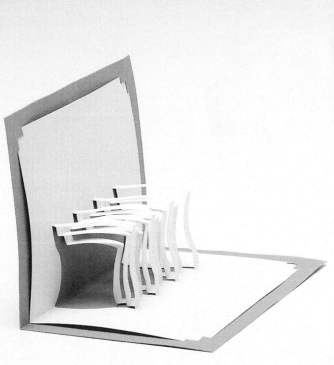

FLOCKS OF BIRDS

CUTTING DIFFICULTY*
FOLDING DIFFICULTY*
MATERIAL USED: 160 gsm RED AND LIGHT BLUE CARDBOARD
DIMENSIONS: 20 X 15 cm EACH

MODEL: PAGE 147
PATTERN TRACING: PAGE 24
CUTTING: PAGE 26
FOLDING: PAGE 27

To make this model, join two cards with a simple 90-degree fold. In the photographs, the two levels are highlighted by the colors red and light blue. In this case, as in the previous one, the design is based on lines and curves. Take care while cutting not to drag the edges with sharp corners with the cutter. This usually happens when the cutter is blunt or when too much pressure is being exerted in the cutting phase. To prevent this from happening, follow the cutting instructions in the "Handy Tips" section.
If you closely observe the photographs or the drawing, you will notice that the folds, although symmetrical to the central one, are not parallel, but converging folds. This is why, seen from the front, the pattern on the red card appears to be made up of lines and not segments as in the previous model.

The graphic effect exerted by this model will be all the more evident if you use very different colors for both levels. On the contrary, to highlight the two flocks of flying birds, try using either a single piece of cardboard folded in half, or cards with two shades of the same color (brown, for example), putting the lighter shade in front and the darker one at the back. To join the two levels together, we chose to glue the two cards, but if you have made the previous model, try using the slotting method described.

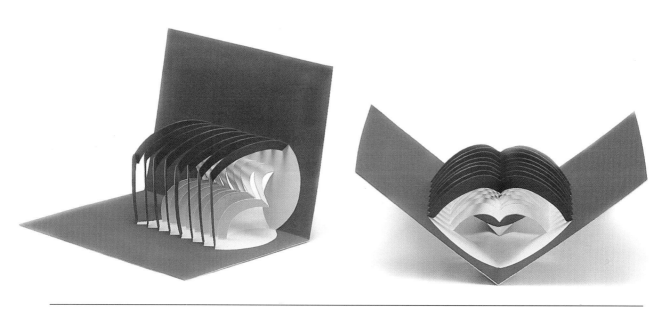

LOTUS FLOWER

CUTTING DIFFICULTY**
FOLDING DIFFICULTY**
MATERIAL USED: 160 gsm YELLOW RECYCLED PIECE OF
CARDBOARD
DIMENSIONS: 20 X 15 cm

MODEL: PAGE 148
PATTERN TRACING: PAGE 24
CUTTING: PAGE 26
FOLDING: PAGE 30

The type of fold used to make this project is a tunnel-type fold of medium difficulty. To understand this model better, look at the photographs: the basic sheet of paper is folded at 90° and the structure is made up of a series of levels. The difference compared to the previous models is that in this case the model is observed with the central fold mountain-wise. In this way, a sort of stage scenery is formed, which the play of light and shade renders particularly attractive. Try to place a source of light behind the sheet of paper and move the model; you will see that it will first resemble an Indian temple illuminated by the rays of the sun, and then a tunnel of plants cleverly cut by a skillful gardener. This type of fold stimulates the observer's imagination and can be used to make full-fledged miniature stage sets, as you will see in the section on objects.
If you find the folds difficult, follow these simple instructions: start by folding the central line mountain-wise; then fold, but not entirely, the mountain lines at the bottom part of the model. Having marked the folds well (in this case we recommend you use the scoring technique), you will find it easy to pinch the sheet of paper into a valley and mountain fold in the upper part of the model.
Make sure you fold gradually, so that the paper takes on the desired shape without too much effort. Flatten and open the model only at the very end, to check the model's movement.

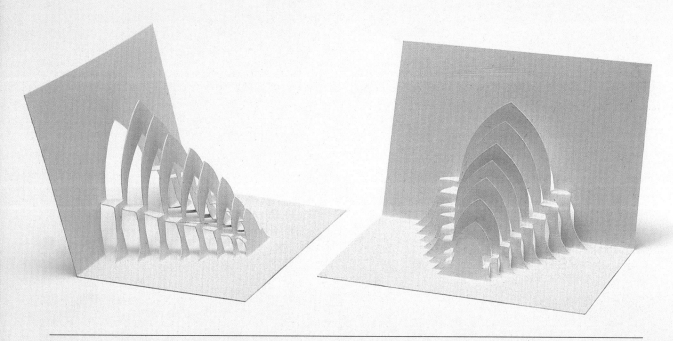

BIRTHDAY CARDS

THE ALPHABET

An alphabet can always come in handy when we're making cards to give or to send as gifts, when wishing to surprise with an animated phrase, or when creating a three-dimensional plaque. There are endless uses. Let your imagination run free with the infinite paper and color combinations possible. Besides the whole alphabet, here is a possible suggestion: a birthday card.
It is a simple 90-degree type with a valley-mountain-valley folding system, but the cut in this case is decidedly more complex compared to that used in the previous model. Should you still feel a little insecure with the cutter, try first to make objects of easy to medium cutting difficulty and only afterwards tackle this model. The instructions set out in the

> CUTTING DIFFICULTY: ***
> FOLDING DIFFICULTY: **
> MATERIAL USED: 160 gsm IVORY AND ORANGE-COLORED CARDBOARDS
> DIMENSIONS: IVORY CARDS: 36 X 14 cm; ORANGE: 37 X 15 cm

following pages will help you to understand how to create and cut the phrase. The most important thing is that you take your time in carrying out the work and that the cuts are sharp, so as to make folding the birthday card quicker and easier.
If you have difficulty in passing your fingers between the letters, try using a pair of tweezers to help you do the folding.
At the end of the folding phase, you will have to choose whether to glue on a backing sheet, so as to increase the surprise effect for the person receiving the card, or you may wish to leave the basic paper free to play with the rays of light coming from every direction.

ABCDEFGHIJKLM

NOPQRSTUVWXYZ

HAPPY BIRTHDAY

Enlarge the drawing of the alphabet 500 percent. Take a sheet of acetate, of the type which architects use for drawing and which can be found in almost all stationers'. Make a rough calculation of the length of the phrase you intend to compose, counting the letters you will need. With a pencil, draw a straight line a little longer than the phrase and start to trace the letters, maintaining this line as a central valley.

Draw the two ends of the model, maintaining the same margins as the template above and below, with a margin of at least one cm on the right and left. Cut out a rectangle similar to the one thus made on the card: in the example proposed, an ivory-colored sheet of paper measuring 36 x 14 cm. Secure the sheet of tracing paper on the template with paper adhesive and place over it an acetate cover in order to trace the inscription.

Try putting the following advice into practice so as to have a copy always handy: make many photocopies of the drawing on the acetate. Now, with a compass, mark the ends of the folding lines and trace the letters. To obtain a good result, it is important that you should take your time. Now remove the two sheets of paper from the foundation cardboard.

Using the scoring technique, mark the mountain folds on the front of the cardboard, and the valley folds on the back, joining the holes previously made with the point of a compass. Cut out the inscription, starting from the innermost parts, that is, from the "empty spaces" in letters such as the "A," "B," or "P." Once you have finished cutting, gently erase the marks left on the tracing paper.

Check that everything has been cut, and start folding from the central valley fold. Should you have any difficulty in doing this, try holding the sheet of paper from the back and inserting your fingers among the letters. Do not fold the central valley fold completely so as not to ruin any of the letters. Remember always to work step-by-step.

Now fold the individual letters starting from the two top and bottom valley lines and then proceed with the mountain line. For the valley folds, try to lift each single letter by pushing with your fingers from the back. Use a pair of tweezers to complete the work.

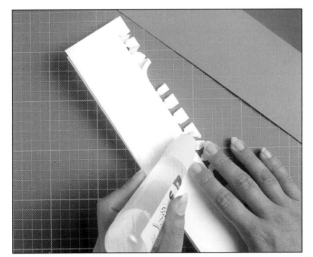

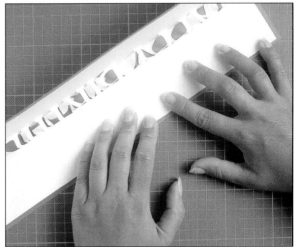

To check whether the folds work, press the sheet of paper and then open it. From a piece of cardboard you wish to use as a backing sheet, cut a rectangle slightly bigger than the actual project card, and fold it in half. In the example depicted in these pages, a 37 x 15 cm rectangle was made from an orange cardboard. Hold the model almost completely folded and spread glue on one half.

Place the glued side of the model along the middle of the backing sheet so that it is equidistant from the borders and the central valley fold coincides with the one on the orange cardboard. Press until well glued and repeat on the other side. In this way, you will obtain the complete model as depicted in the previous pages.

A HEART

CUTTING DIFFICULTY: *
FOLDING DIFFICULTY: **
MATERIAL USED: 160 gsm IVORY CARDBOARD AND RED RICE
PAPER
DIMENSIONS: 20 X 15 cm EACH
RED TEMPERA

MODEL: PAG 148
TRACING: PAGE 24
CUTTING: PAGE 26
FOLDING: PAGE 27
APPLYNG THE BACKING SHEET: PAGE 32
DECORATING: PAGE 36

Here is a simple model that can be used on several occasions. The double heart may be enriched with the use of special paper, such as red rice paper which contains silk threads (illustrated in these photographs), or by using decorations such as the spray technique proposed here. In order to heighten the contrast between colors, the background can be made greater in relation to the foundation sheet. This is not advisable if you are using a very light sheet of paper, because it would not hold the weight of the entire model.

Folding this model is quite simple. After having made the central valley, partly fold the large heart and then the internal one, pushing it back with your finger.

After folding, glue the base while holding the ground sheet at 90 degrees. Make sure you use very little glue and that you spread it well, as rice paper is very porous and dark stains could easily occur. Once these form, they cannot be removed.

When the glue has dried, prepare the colors to be used for decorating the model.

Use a copy of the project pattern to make a stencil that will allow you to spray color only onto the heart, and not onto the rest of the foundation. Remember to fold the model only when the color has completely dried throughout, so as not to cause unwanted staining.

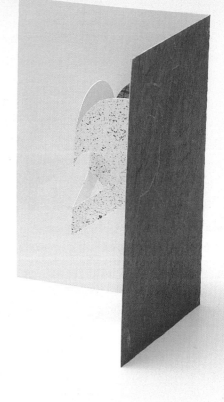

A FLOWER

CUTTING DIFFICULTY: **
FOLDING DIFFICULTY: *
MATERIAL USED: 160 gsm LILAC CARDBOARD
AND 220 gsm BRIGHT GREEN CARDBOARD
DIMENSIONS: 10 X 15 cm (LILAC); 11 X 16 cm (GREEN)

MODEL: PAGE 148
TRACING: PAGE 24
CUTTING: PAGE 26
FOLDING: PAGE 31
APPLYNG BACKING SHEET: PAGE 32
DECORATING: PAGE 39

This card uses the 180-degree slotted fold. The petals of the flower cut out from the ground sheet need to be wound around each other in order to create the effect depicted in the photographs. The folding system is very straightforward: first, fold the paper in two along the valley section; then raise the flowers by folding the bases of their stems valley-wise.

The cut is a little more complex and requires some experience, because the design is made up of a series of straight lines with very small rays. Try as much as possible to avoid lifting the cutter from the cardboard when going over the curves. This will ensure that the design's contours are continuous rather than segmented. This is one of those instances in which we advise using a scalpel rather than a cutter. If sufficiently sharp, the scalpel's blade will make it easier to follow the curved lines.

Before cutting and folding, remember to mark the folds (in this case creasing is enough) and to use the metal tip or a compass to make the small holes at the center of the flower, as in the pattern.

At this point, fold the leaves slightly in order to give them a more natural look. To give the model a nice finish, use a different-colored background (in the photographs, a grassy green). A background is not necessary for the stability of this project, but it does heighten the surprise effect and increases the sturdiness of the flat section.

CHRISTMAS CARDS

CUTTING DIFFICULTY: *
FOLDING DIFFICULTY: **
MATERIAL USED: 160 gsm RED, WHITE AND GREEN CARDBOARD
DIMENSIONS: 20 X 5 cm EACH

MODEL: PAG 149
TRACING: PAG 24
CUTTING: PAG 26
FOLDING: PAGE 28

This proposal makes use of three different objects which, in their form and color, are typical of the symbolism linked to Christmas and the New Year: the tree, the star, and the candle. These cards can be used to add originality to your gift wraps. Should you use cardboard that is up to 20 cm thick, rather than 5 cm as proposed here, you can use these models as Christmas greetings. The structure of each of these cards is based on a zero fold. The valley formed becomes the basis for depicting the three objects as though they were 90-degree models. The relative simplicity of these models owes more to their small dimensions than to the type of fold used.

The tree is formed by a number of parallel cuts, which are connected by converging symmetrical folds to the central valley. You will find a detailed description of the necessary folding technique in the next section (Fir Trees), which is based on the model of a tree.

The candles, on the other hand – as you will see from the photographs – are arranged on two different levels that are asymmetrical to the basic valley fold. Be particularly careful in cutting out the flames: start from the candle and continue up towards the tip on either side. In this way, you will avoid ruining the flame tips by dragging them while you cut. To fold, start from the central valley, then fold the left candle and finally the right one.

As the star has a number of acute angles, it is a little more difficult to make. Follow the instructions given above. Or follow the tips provided on page 34. To fold the model, start from the central valley, then fold the outside star, and finally push the internal one inward. Remember to follow these instructions step-by-step, being careful not to tear the connecting strips between the stars and their background.

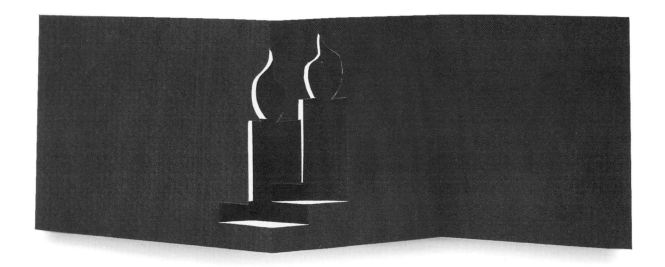

FIR TREES

A few parallel cuts and converging folds are enough to create a group of fir trees from a piece of cardboard. The material used is especially important in this case.

CUTTING DIFFICULTY: *
FOLDING DIFFICULTY: **
MATERIAL USED: 200 gsm COTTON PAPER WITH LINEN THEARDS
DIMENSIONS: 30 X 15 cm

MODEL: PAG 150
TRACING: PAGE 24
CUTTING: PAG 26
FOLDING: PAG 27

repeated three times on a card. The cuts are formed by a series of parallel straight lines, and thus are very easy to make. The folds are slightly more complex but, once

Small linen threads in a green card can create the illusion of snowflakes falling in a forest, while also softening the linearity of this type of design. This model can be used as a card, but also as a small stage set. Placing a small, low-wattage lamp behind the card creates a certain atmosphere. As light is also a source of heat, however, make sure that the lamp is not in direct contact with the card, allowing enough space for air to pass between the two. As an extra precaution, do not leave the light on for too long in order to prevent the card from burning.

The structure is equivalent to a 90-degree model

learned, only need to be repeated three times. Start by making the two longest mountain folds, in order to see clearly how much space is available for each fir tree. Then fold the central valley of the first tree. By pressing with your fingers from behind the cardboard, gently bend the strips representing the treetop and branches. The top is the most difficult section to bend, as it is the most resistant to folding. Insist a little by using a finger to press from behind the card, and your free hand to press the valley sections on the front of the model. Close well, then open up the first fir tree again, and repeat for the remaining two.

PAYSAGE DE NOEL

CUTTING DIFFICULTY: **
FOLDING DIFFICULTY: **
MATERIAL USED: 160 gsm, DEEP BLUE CARDBOARD
DIMENSIONS: 20 X 15 cm

MODEL: PAGE 149
TRACING: PAGE 24
CUTTING: PAGE 26
FOLDING: PAGE 28
DECORATING: PAGE 39

Small-scale architecture, the fruit of fantasy, and a starry night sky, instantly conjure up images of the Three Kings' journey. In order to represent this subject, we have chosen a 90-degree model made from a card without any background. The design is divided into two sections: one, on the left, with symmetrical folds to the central valley; and the other, on the right, made up of a symmetrical part (the main body of the building) and built-on part (the stairs).

The model is graded medium difficulty because of the presence of curved sections, with rays' radii of varying width. Besides this, the sectioning technique is particularly apparent here. Both the doors and the cupolas of the buildings are in fact cut beyond the fold line (valley for the doors and mountain for the cupolas). When tracing the model, use a compass to mark off the stars. Once the cutting and scoring operations have been completed, simply widen the holes with the compass tip to obtain the effect you can see in the photographs.

First cut the curves, and then the straight lines; this makes it easier to connect the former to the latter while correcting any small mistakes that might have occurred. Begin folding from the central valley, and continue with the left section and the top valley of the right one.

Fold the steps one by one by pushing from behind with your fingers, and finally complete the fold.

FOR THE LITTLE ONES

CIRCUS

CUTTING DIFFICULTY***
FOLDING DIFFICULTY**
MATERIALS: 160 gsm WHITE AND RED CARDBOARD
DIMENSIONS: 40 X 30 WHITE CARD; 28 X 28 CM RED CARD
WATERCOLORS

The group of projects described in these pages are designed for small children. These models, in fact, can either be used as birthday cards or as "toys" with which they can play. Because making these projects requires the use of a cutter, we do not recommend you let the children do the cutting. To teach the younger ones the art of Kirigami, other materials, not specified in this manual, are usually used, such as a pair of scissors in place of a cutter.

Described on the following pages, are projects that highlight the expressive possibilities of the materials used and the different decorations that can be created from them, from white watercolor paper to soft papers, to bright-colored ones. These differences will certainly stimulate children's curiosity. Welcome to the circus! the manager, the clowns, and the acrobats are here to greet you. You can also catch a glimpse of the lion and the elephant. This is a 180-degree model with a relatively complex pattern, particularly with regards to the cutting procedures. This is why a thorough, step-by-step explanation is given on the following pages, that will prove useful while carrying out the project. This model requires a compact, uniform type of paper, such as mass-produced paper, which is easy to cut. It does not necessarily require decoration, but a touch of color, no matter how delicate, will help children understand the model better and also make it more attractive.

Enlarge the template of the circus by 150 percent. Cut out
a 40 x 30 cm rectangle from a piece of white cardboard.
Using paper adhesive, attach a piece of tracing paper and
the photocopy to the ground sheet. With the point of a
compass, mark the ends of the folds and the eyes of the
characters.

Carefully trace the whole pattern, except for the folding
lines, with a hard-pointed pencil; the latter will allow you to
trace the pattern well without dirtying the photocopy or your
hands very much.

Remove the photocopy and the tracing paper. Mark the
folds with the line folder, pressing the valley part, as
indicated in the picture, or scoring the mountain fold with
the cutter. Choose the technique that is best suited to the
type of card used.

Start cutting from the innermost lines, such as the
elephant's eyes and the character's faces. Turn to pages
34 and 35 for some tips on cutting circles and the lion's
mane.

Once you have finished cutting, you will notice that certain parts of the card need to be removed completely. Check that the whole drawing has been properly cut and that the marks left on the piece of cardboard by the tracing paper have been accurately erased.

Now start folding the model. Should you prefer decorating the model before folding it, read through the last paragraph on page 80 and come back to this paragraph once your model has completely dried. Lift the characters slightly and fold the elephant's body mountain-wise.

Continue by folding valley-wise the bases of characters along one side of the circus. Should you have any difficulty in carrying this out, use a pair of tweezers. Then fold mountain- and valley-wise, thus distancing the different shapes from each other.

Turn the sheet of paper over and repeat this whole operation on the other side of the circus. Slightly bend certain parts of the model outward, such as the clowns' ribbons and noses, the elephant's ears, and the lion's mane. To do this, lift the parts that need bending with the help of the cutter.

Now take the red, square-shaped piece of card and, with a compass, draw a circle 27 cm in diameter. Cut the circle without ever lifting the cutter off the card, in order to obtain a perfect curve. Fold it in half, marking the diameter valley-wise.

Attach the two bases of the model to the red card, making sure the straight lines in the middle of the drawing run parallel to each other, and that they are each a couple of millimeters away from the circle's central valley fold. This will make opening and closing the model easier.

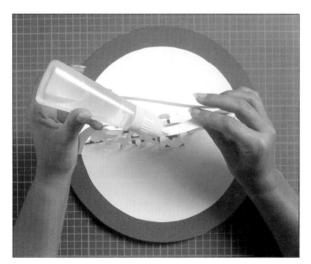

Fold the two arches of the model towards the center and glue in such a way as to evoke a somewhat stylised marquee. With a drop of glue, attach the two parts of the elephant's trunk and the lion's snout together.

Color the character's mustaches, noses, and ribbons, along with most of the animals. If you choose to decorate the model once folded, the warping caused by watercolors creates an interesting three-dimensional effect.

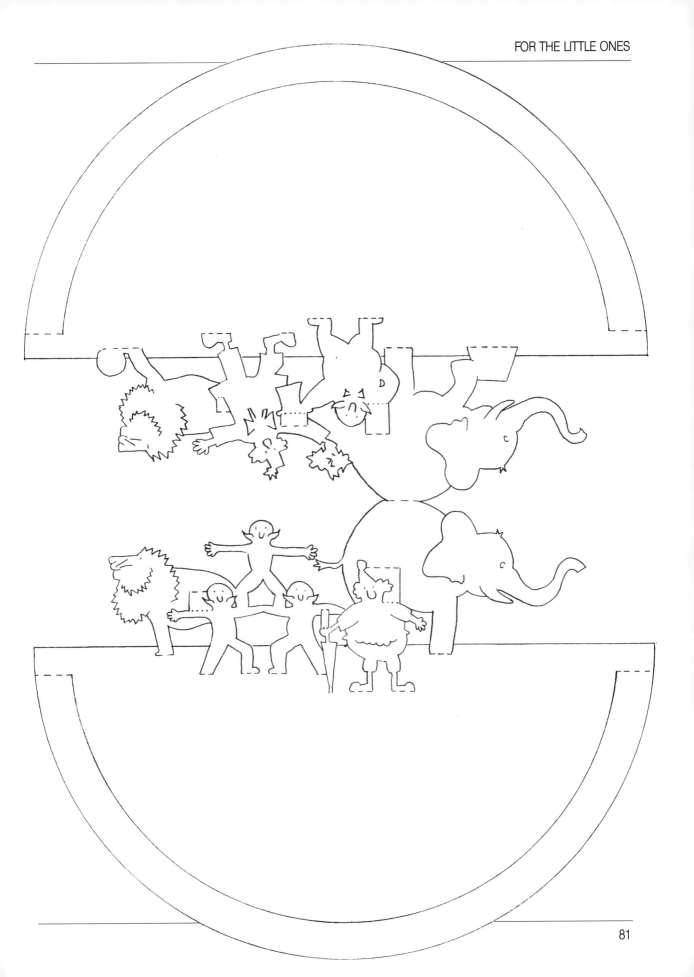

BEAR CUBES

CUTTING DIFFICULTY*
FOLDING DIFFICULTY*
MATERIALS: 200 gsm IVORY RICE PAPER AN BROWN,
LINEN-THEARDED COTTON PAPER
DIMENSIONS: 20 X 15 cm EACH

MODEL: PAGE 151
TRACING: PAGE 24
CUTTING: PAGE 26
FOLDING: PAGE 27
APPLYNG A BACKING SHEET: PAGE 32

Teddies are among children's best-loved toys. This model evokes their outline in a simple and easily made way. It is a 90-degree model, symmetrical to the central fold, consists of only a few lines, and can also be made by younger children. The sense of touch here is of the utmost importance. You can use any type of cardboard, because the model presents no cutting or folding difficulties whatsoever. The model depicted on these pages was made with cotton, linen-threaded paper, which renders it soft to the touch and slightly textured. The threads that randomly appear across the surface give the model a greater sense of lightness and softness.

To make this project, follow the standard procedure. If you decide to use soft paper, score the folds, making them less rigid.
To make the eyes and the belly button perfectly rounded, follow the instructions on page 35 or prick the card with the point of a compass and then widen the holes as for "A Christmas Landscape."
Fold the model, starting from the central valley fold and continuing with the side ones. Finally, secure a backing sheet to the model if desired. If you intend using rice paper, as was used for the model in the photographs, apply very little glue and spread well so as to prevent the surface from staining.

CHILDREN

CUTTING DIFFICULTY***
FOLDING DIFFICULTY**
MATERIALS: 160 gsm COTTON PAPER WITH VEGETABLE FIBERES
AND GREEN CARDBOARD
DIMENSIONS: COTTON: 19 X 14 cm;
GREEN CARDBOARD: 20 X 15 cm
MODEL: PAGE 151
TRACING: PAGE 24
CUTTING: PAGE 26
FOLDING: PAGE 31

In this model, a boy and a girl hold hands thanks to a simple play of slots. This is, in fact, a 180-degree slotted model. While cutting may be a little difficult, folding is really simple: all you need do is fold the central line and the feet of the two characters valley-wise. To block the model into its final position, interlock the slits in the children's hands.

As with the previous model, the type of paper used influences the end result considerably. Using a soft piece of cardboard with vegetable inlays softens the lines in the drawing and reminds us of two children playing in a field. The musk-green backing sheet accentuates this effect and creates an interesting play with the cut-out sections of the project card. This is the illusion of the children's shadow, albeit somewhat improbable, as each "shadow" falls in an opposite direction. This effect is emphasized by the presence of a dark background, but can be camouflaged if two sheets of paper of the same color are used.

Remember to cut the backing sheet in half before gluing it, in order to make it easier to open the 180-degree model completely. To make the characters' ribbons and noses more evident, remember to lift these off the card slightly, with the use of a cutter, or push them forward with the tip of the line folder.

SMALL CARS

CUTTING DIFFICULTY**
FOLDING DIFFICULTY**
MATERIALS: 160 gsm RED CARDBOARD
AND 200 gsm YELLOW CARDBOARD
DIMENSIONS: 15 X 27 cm RED CARBOARD;
20 X 15 cm YELLOW CARDBOARD
MODEL: PAGE 152
TRACING: PAGE 24
CUTTING: PAGE 26
FOLDING: PAGE 31
APPLYNG A BACKING SHEET: PAGE 32

Cars are also especially adored by children. In this model, they are ready to leave as soon as the lights turn green. The model is a combination between a simple 180-degree type, for the cars, and a slotted one, for the traffic lights. This means that the final structure will be more than a normal 180-degree one; nevertheless, it will still be necessary to use a backing sheet in order to hold the figures in place securely.

The contrast between the red used for the model and the yellow color of the backing sheet will make the model all the more attractive to children. With a little imagination, you will realize that the traffic light cutouts have become the cars' finishing line. As with all models of this type you will need to remove from the foundation cardboard all those areas that are not part of the subject. Remember to mark the folds clearly and start folding from the roof of the middle car. Then fold each side of the car mountain- and valley-wise, and later slot in the two traffic light segments. Mark the central valley of the foundation cardboard and glue it to the model, in such a way that the two parts that will form the road plane are one or two millimeters away from the central valley fold of the base. When you are done, you have a new toy!

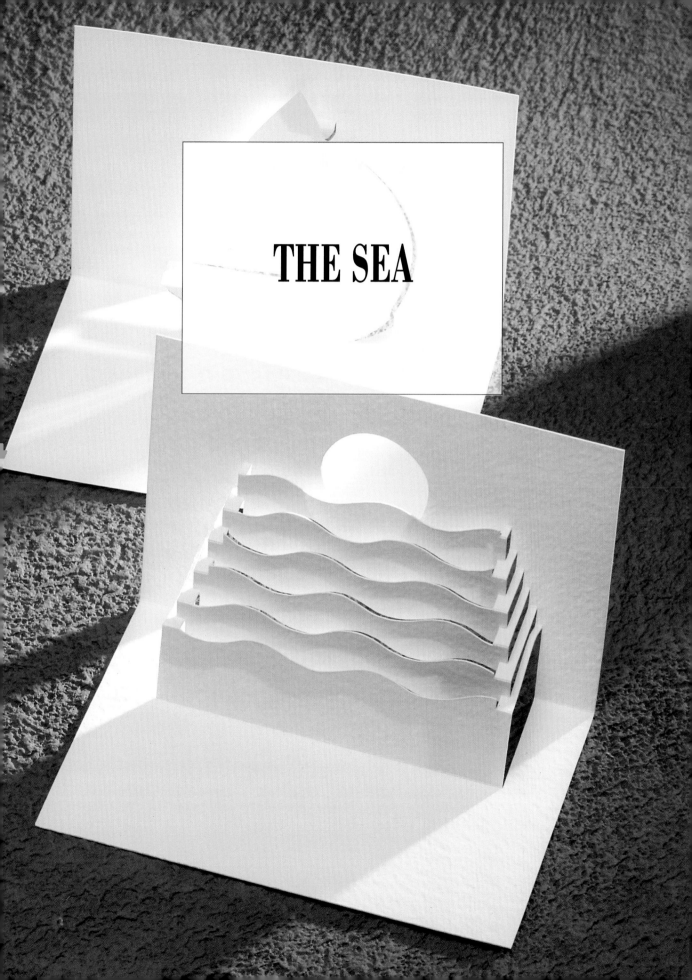

THE SEA

FISH

CUTTING DIFFICULTY***
FOLDING DIFFICULTY**
MATERIALS: 160 gsm BLUE AND LIGHT BLUE CARDBOARD
DIMENSIONS: 20 X 15 cm EACH
COLORED TEMPERA

A small school of well-rounded fish, with a reassuring expression, swim through a light blue sea. By playing with shadows and moving the cardboard, the group of fish grows in number, then shrinks back to the original three. This 90-degree model has a number of specific characteristics: the cutting of small curves, the use of small circles such as those for the eyes, the use of spray decoration. For these reasons, you will find step-by-step instructions to help you out. The folds are, on the other hand, relatively simple: they run parallel to the central valley and the fish are laid out on three different levels, as can be seen in the photographs.

Should you like to color in the models, there are a variety of suitable decorations you could use. Tempera, watercolor, felt pen and pencil are the most common. By using a little imagination you will be able to create all kinds of cards, with colored or white fish, different or similar ones, smooth or with scales.

For the time being, try out this model by following the instructions given in the next few pages. When you feel confident, get creative.

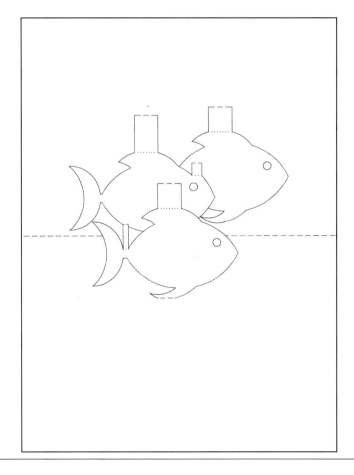

Trace the drawing for the model, attaching a photocopy (enlarged by 175 percent) and the graph paper to the blue cardboard. Remember to mark the end of the folding line with a compass. After removing the photocopy, start marking the mountain folds by scoring the front of the card. Turn the sheet of cardboard over and mark the mountain folds for this side of the cardboard, again by scoring.

Start cutting from the innermost sections of the drawing. Be particularly careful in cutting the round sections for the eyes: should you not obtain the desired results, follow the tips listed on pages 34 and 35. Remember that it is best not to lift the cutter off the card until you have finished cutting a line, be it straight or curved.

Before folding, check that the cutting has been precisely executed and that the fins' and tails' corners lift off the card. As with all 90-degree models, begin folding from the central valley line, lifting out the fish figures with your fingers. Remember that the folds need to be made in successive stages.

Fold the following valley-wise: the fin connecting the first fish to the card, then the spacers between other fish and the backing sheet. Now make the three larger mountain folds and the two smaller ones by moving your hands in a fashion similar to that depicted in the photograph. Having marked the fold lines by scoring, you will notice that the card easily responds to your movements.

Once folding has been completed, cut out the fish from the photocopy used in the first step. You may either keep or discard the two upper spacers. Take the cut photocopy, fold it along the central valley, and lay it on the card, making sure that the paper both covers and adheres to the card. Keep the sheets folded at 90 degrees and do not flatten them.

Dilute the red and yellow tempera in two separate basins. The color must be liquid, but not watery. Dip the toothbrush in the red basin and start spraying. If you are unfamiliar with this technique, follow the instructions on page 36. Rinse the toothbrush thoroughly in water, and use again to spray on the yellow tempera. In this way the yellow droplets will be more visible, as they will be highlighted against the red background.

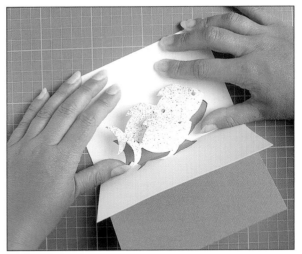

Allow the color to dry for about ten minutes. Remove the template and check for unwanted marks on the foundation sheet. If you are satisfied with the results, prepare the blue cardboard that will be used for the model's backing sheet. Fold valley-wise along half the length of the shorter side of this last sheet and then reopen it.

Leave the foundation sheet of paper folded at 90 degrees, and spread glue over the back of the upper half. In this way, you will avoid gluing the fish and spacers together — these must remain free. Lay the light blue card on the blue one so that the central valley folds coincide. Press down and hold for a few seconds. Repeat this operation for the lower half. If necessary, trim the edges once everything has been securely glued together.

DOLPHINS

CUTTING DIFFICULTY**
FOLDING DIFFICULTY*
MATERIALS: 160 gsm CARDBOARD AND 100 gsm IVORY PAPER
DIMENSIONS: 20 X 15 cm FOR TWO SHEETS OF BLUE
CARDBOARD; 19 X 14 cm IVORY PAPER BLUE
BLUE INDIAN INK

MODEL: PAGE 153
TRACING: PAGE 24
CUTTING: PAGE 26-34
FOLDING: PAGE 28
APPLYNG A BACKING SHEET: PAGE 32
DECORATION: PAGE 38

One, two or three dolphins? Here light and shadow play off the paper, doubling the image of a dolphin leaping through sea spray. This model is the most complicated version: besides the blue foundation sheet, there are also a blue backing sheet and a decorated template. The backing sheet and decoration are not necessary, but serve to heighten the doubling effect.

From a technical point of view, the model consists of very simple folds (90-degree converging folds), but is a little more complex as regards cutting. Be particularly careful with the fins and seaspray, for which we advise you to refer to the tips listed on page 34.

Once you have cut out the dolphin from the foundation paper, you can add a similar or different-colored backing sheet and choose whether to decorate the subject. If you intend making the model presented here, use an absorbent paper (or one of a similar kind) and decorate it by using the *Suminagashi* technique. In order to achieve this particular marbled ink effect, turn to the instructions on page 38. Once the sheet of paper has dried completely, cut out a 14 x 19 cm rectangle. Cut out the dolphin and glue the resulting template to the foundation paper. Finally, add a backing sheet that is similar in color to the foundation paper. In this way, you will achieve the same effect as that illustrated in the photographs. Or, design your own background to give yours an original feeling.

SAILING BOAT

CUTTING DIFFICULTY**
FOLDING DIFFICULTY**
MATERIALS: 160 gsm LIGHT BLUE AND AQUAMARINE
CARDBOARD
DIMENSIONS: 20 X 15 cm EACH

MODEL: PAGE 153
TRACING: PAGE 24
CUTTING: PAGE 26
FOLDING: PAGE 28
APPLYNG A BACKING SHEET: PAGE 32

After having looked at fish and dolphins, we now move to the sea's surface, where suddenly a sailing boat appears, its sails fully unfurled by the winds. You will clearly see from the lateral view that this is a 90-degree model, built on three layers with folds running parallel to the central valley. This allows us to clearly distinguish the three segments that constitute the model: the boat, the front sail, and the back one.

When observing a boat from some distance, it is often difficult to pick out its colors. It appears to be a uniform light blue, almost faded, color. This is why we have chosen a light blue card, with a smooth surface, as the foundation sheet for this model.

The type of cut is not difficult: the curves are quite gentle and the tips of the two sails present the only acute angles. When folding, try to stick to the following order: first fold the central valley, then the boat, and finally the sails. Remember always to proceed gradually, step-by-step, so as to avoid causing unwanted folds. Should you have difficulty in folding the connectors between the sails, try using a pair of tweezers, but make sure you don't push the cardboard too far. Once you have finished the model, you can choose whether or not to use a backing sheet. This is not needed in making the card, but can be used to create special effects.

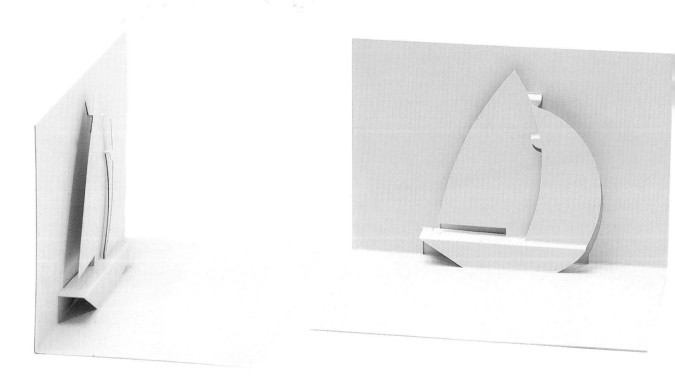

SUNSET ON THE SEA

CUTTING DIFFICULTY**
FOLDING DIFFICULTY***
MATERIALS: 200 gsm, LIGHT BLUE COTTON MOONROCK PAPER
DIMENSIONS: 20 X 15 cm EACH

MODEL: PAGE 154
TRACING: PAGE 24
CUTTING: PAGE 26
FOLDING: PAGE 28-29

How wonderful to observe a sunset over a paper sea, and to discover that the waves, laid out on several levels, move and appear doubled thanks to a play of light between the different levels!

The paper used here is particularly crucial, perhaps more so than for other models. We advise that you choose cardboard with a large grain somewhere in between a white, light blue, and blue color. Cotton and watercolor paper are suitable.

The models in these photographs have been made with moonrock card. This type of card is soft and its surface sponge-like, thus emphasizing the model's main characteristics. The sense of airiness, emphasized by light filtering through the different levels, is maintained by not using a backing sheet.

This 90-degree model is made up of six levels that are all connected to each other and to the foundation sheet. When cutting and folding, follow these few tips. Select a method for marking the folds in relation to the type of card that you have chosen: for a soft card, use the creasing technique; for a hard card, use the scoring one. First cut the curved sections, then the straight lines, so as to avoid tearing one of the strips connecting the waves to one another.

When folding, remember to start from the central fold and from the foot of the sea. If you have clearly marked the folds, you will notice that the cardboard automatically takes on its final shape, almost without your help.

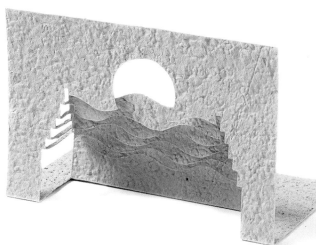

ARCHITECTURE

WINDOW OVERLOOKING PARIS

CUTTING DIFFICULTY***
FOLDING DIFFICULTY***
MATERIALS: 160 gsm, LIGHT YELLOW AND BLUE CARDBOARD
DIMENSIONS: 20 X 15 cm BLUE CARDBOARD;
19,6 X 26,6 CM LIGHT YELLOW CARDBOARD

Open your window and there in front of you, hidden by a slight morning mist, are the rooftops of Paris, with the Eiffel Tower in the distance.

This model consists of two separate 90-degree sections: the window, made with yellow cardboard, and the Parisian sky-line, made with blue. The two sections can be glued to each other so as to form one object, or they can be easily slotted in and out of each other. Should you want to pursue the latter option, read the instructions on page 32. For this model, as with all architectural ones, use 160 gsm stiff, compacted card, or as heavy a card as will allow you to obtain precise cuts and clear folds. Both the window and skyline are complete models, and can therefore be made independently of each other. The window is made up of a simple parallelepiped, which emerges from the backing sheet thanks to one mountain and two valley folds. The Parisian skyline, is a little more complex, on the other hand, as it is formed by three different levels, connected to each other and to the backing sheet in order to create a perspectival effect. Cutting is also more complicated than that needed for the window. The roofs' profiles and other architectural elements are formed by curved lines and by parallel and converging straight lines. Now turn to the instructions listed on the following pages, and proceed step-by-step in order to create both models individually, as well as the combined one.

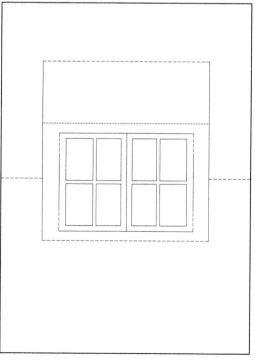

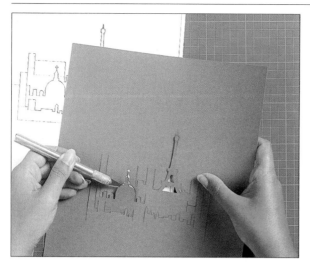

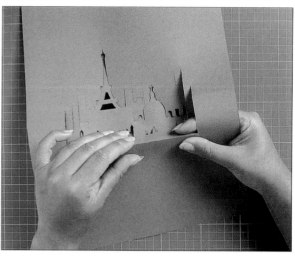

Following the procedure you already know, copy the drawing of the Paris skyline (enlarged by 286 percent) on blue cardboard measuring 20 x 27 cm. Then score the section that is mountain-side of the folds, by using a scorer, and cut by starting with the innermost sections of the drawing and the curved lines. Check that all the parts of the model have been cut by lifting them with the cutter; and erase any marks left by the graph paper.

Fold by starting with the central valley and the longer valley at the foot of the skyline. To make things easier, turn the card over and fold these lines from behind, as depicted in the photograph. Continue with the valley lines that connect the Eiffel Tower to the backing sheet, and then with the innermost mountain and valley ones.

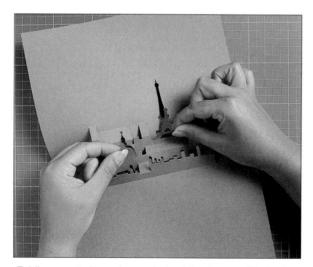

Folding must always be carried out by degrees. Each step is a necessary one, and it brings you closer to the final product. In order to separate the different levels, lightly grip the second and third levels with either hand and delicately move them in opposite directions, so that the mountain and valley folds form between them. Repeat to obtain the folds between the first and second levels.

Once all lines mountain- and valley-side have been folded, at least to 90 degrees, flatten the card so that the model opens and closes smoothly. Be very careful when doing this, and avoid folding the chimney tops, the cross, and other protruding elements. Open to check that everything is as it should be.

Cut a 19.6 x 26.6 cm rectangle from the yellow cardboard, and glue it to a photocopy of the window (also enlarged by 286 percent). In this instance, you will not need to use graph paper to copy the model: all you need to do is make a slight hole at either end of each line with a compass. Mark the folds, cut, and check the cut by lifting the eight rectangles off the window to form the window panes.

Now fold the drawing. As there are only one mountain and two valley folds, this should be quite simple. Open both frames of the window by pulling them towards you, and close them again in such a way that they appear slightly ajar, each open to a different degree. You will open and shut the windows many times, particularly once the model has been fully folded and reopened.

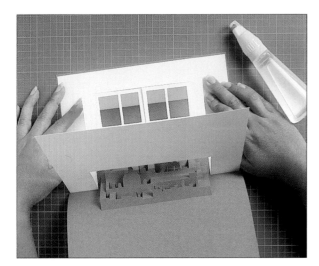

Spread non-vinyl glue on the back of the upper half of the yellow cardboard, so as to stick the backing sheet of the card to the blue card and leave the window free. Center this section over the upper half of the blue cardboard, in such a way that each card's central valley folds correlate (as shown in the photograph); press well.

Repeat for the other half, making sure that you don't completely flatten the two layers. Make sure that glue does not spread beyond the cardboards' edges. Open and close the model a number of times before the glue dries completely, so as to check that it works properly. If necessary, trim the edges with a cutter so that they run parallel to each other.

NEW YORK SKY-SCRAPERS

CUTTING DIFFICULTY***
FOLDING DIFFICULTY***
MATERIALS: 160 gsm RAF BLUE CARDBOARD
DIMENSIONS: 23 X 30 cm

MODEL: PAGE 155
TRACING: PAGE 24
CUTTING: PAGE 26
FOLDING: PAGE 28

This is how Lower Manhattan's skyscrapers appear when viewed from the Hudson River or from the Statue of Liberty. Two elements in this skyline are particularly recognizable. At its center are the twin towers of the World Trade Center, each 110 floors high, while to the left lie the World Financial Center buildings, whose roofs have different geometric shapes. Farther ahead, almost in the shadow of these skyscrapers, one can make out the low silhouettes of the older buildings that face the river and look out towards the Statue of Liberty. This is where the famous Wall Street is located.

This is a multi-level, 90-degree model, obtained from a single sheet of cardboard. The forms that shape the skyline are asymmetrical to the central valley, and are strictly connected to each other. In order to achieve a good result, clearly trace the folds mountain-side, and cut the model with the aid of a metal ruler. The cutting difficulty is caused primarily by the length of the whole operation, rather than by the presence of complex lines. The most complicated part of this model is the folding. Start with the central valley fold and continue with the valleys connecting the skyscrapers, the sky, and the river. In this way, the mountain folds will tend to fall into place automatically. Continue with these operations step-by-step, starting from the twin towers' mountain folds, and gradually increase pressure on the folds. With a little patience, you will achieve an excellent result.

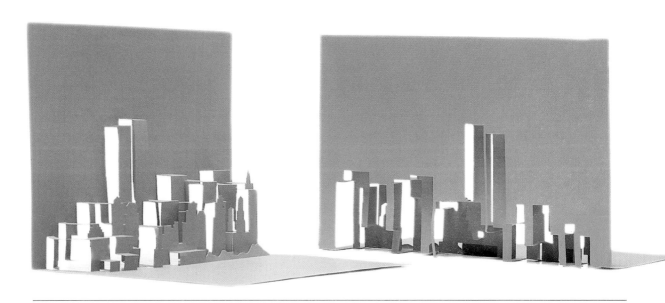

TOWER BRIDGE

CUTTING DIFFICULTY***
FOLDING DIFFICULTY***
MATERIALS: 160 gsm CREAM AND DARK BLUE CARDBOARD
DIMENSIONS: 23 X 30 cm EACH
MODEL: PAGE 155
TRACING: PAGE 24
CUTTING: PAGE 26
FOLDING: PAGE 31
APPLYNG A BACKING SHEET: PAGE 32

London's Tower Bridge was opened in 1874 and has been considered one of the symbols of the city ever since. The bridge has a central mobile section that allows large ships to sail through. Until 1976 the drawbridge was activated by a steam motor that dated back to the Victorian age, but this has since then been replaced by the use of electricity.

In the paper model presented in these pages, the drawbridge opens and closes thanks to four oblique folds, which join in pairs at two opposite ends of the central valley line. This causes the central section of the model to rise every time the model is closed, and to be lowered every time it is opened.

The two spiked towers and the connecting walkway (which provides passers-by with a stunning view over the River Thames) have been cut out from the foundation card. This is a 180-degree model and uses the gluing technique rather than the slotted one.

After having traced the model and cut out the shapes from the card, first fold the drawbridge and then the foot of the towers. Secure the peaks of the two towers with a drop of glue and connect the blue backing sheet.

Remember to cut the dark blue backing card in half along the central line (which serves as a support for the model, but is not essential) and then secure it, so as to make it easier to open the foundation card to 180 degrees.

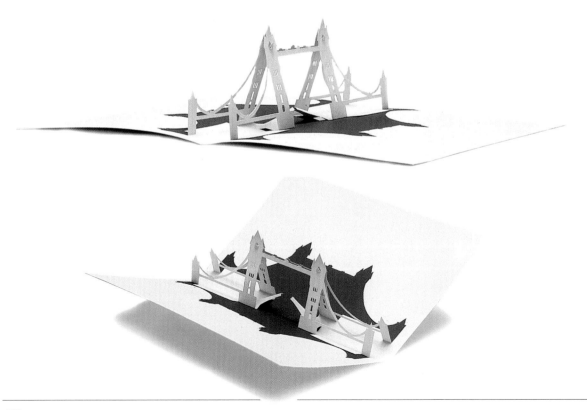

FENIS CASTLE

CUTTING DIFFICULTY***
FOLDING DIFFICULTY***
MATERIALS: 160 gsm LIGHT LIGHT MUSTARD-COLORED CARD
DIMENSIONS: 23 X 30 cm
MODEL: PAGE 156
TRACING: PAGE 24
CUTTING: PAGE 26
FOLDING: PAGE 28

The model depicted on these pages is a stylized version of the Fénis Castle in Val d'Aosta, Italy. This old manor house was built in the second half of the 14th century and today ranks as one of the most interesting and best preserved examples of medieval defense architecture.

From the outside, the castle looks hostile and severe, sporting a double embattled defense wall overlooked by a series of towers. From the inside, on the other hand, it is a welcoming and peaceful dwelling place, with a series of balconies surrounding an inner courtyard, and characterized by numerous picturesque elements.

Like the real castle, the paper model also has a dual nature. The castle is made of a series of different planes and volumes, and its defense element is omnipresent. In the example depicted here, it is made with a pale, mustard-colored card. Place it close to a source of light — when back-lit, the model takes on different colors and undergoes a subtle transformation. Score the folds before cutting the pattern. Pay particular attention to the two embattled walls. We recommend cutting the curved parts first, then the oblique ones, and finally the parallel section (first the longitudinal ones and then the transversal ones). Now start the 90-degree fold from the central fold, from the two valley folds of the hill, and from the first embattled boundary wall. Continue with the valley folds connecting the second crenellated wall to the foundation card and then with the longer mountain folds. In this way you shouldn't have any difficulty in folding the remaining lines and obtaining the final shape.

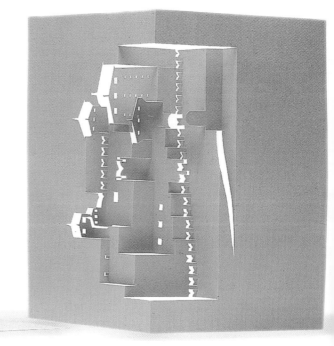

SAN LORENZO

CUTTING DIFFICULTY***
FOLDING DIFFICULTY***
MATERIALS: 160 gsm CORN-COLORED CARDBOARD
DIMENSIONS: 23 X 30 cm
MODEL: PAGE 156
TRACING: PAGE 24
CUTTING: PAGE 26
FOLDING: PAGE 28

The chapels and towers of the Basilica of San Lorenzo, overlooking the Piazza Vetra in Milan, are the starting point for one of the most interesting and complex models described in this manual.

San Lorenzo is one of the most important Milanese monuments, a paleochristian basilica that dates back to the 5th century. It is designed on a square plant and is enriched by its chapels. It underwent restoration in the late 14th century. Eight different levels were needed in order to create the complexity of the bulk that overlooks the square at the back of the church. This project is best suited to those of you who are already hands at this craft.

The complexity is mainly due to the many openings that require curved and straight cuts. To obtain a good result, read the paragraph on cutting curved lines on page 35. Once you have cut the pattern, you will notice that every level is interlinked with the next, and either directly or indirectly to the background. For greater ease, carry out precise folding steps. Start, as usual, with the central valley fold, followed immediately by the valley folds at the foot of the pattern. Then gradually fold, mountain- and valley-wise, the space between the cupola and the background. Continue with the mountain and valley lines of the different levels until you get to the first one. At this point, fold the two sides of the main cardboard until the model is complete.

OBJECTS

PENCIL HOLDER

CUTTING DIFFICULTY*
FOLDING DIFFICULTY**
MATERIALS: GREEN MOONROCK PAPER
OR WHITE WATERCOLOR PAPER
DIMENSIONS: 20 X 50 cm

The objects described in this section pertain to three groups. The first is a desk set, the second Christmas decorations, and the third children's toys. The first group consists of a pencil holder, a floppy disk holder, a pocket telephone book, and a lamp.

The pencil holder depicted on this page is easy to make and always comes in handy. It is made with a single sheet of paper forming a pair of parallelepiped entirely, thanks to a play of slots. No glue, tape, or any other type of adhesive is required. This is why the pencil holder can be flattened and rebuilt whenever required; it can be presented as a gift or transported empty so that it doesn't take up too much space. They are surprisingly sturdy.

The end object consists of two containers, of different heights, connected to each other by a strip used for slotting that can be used to lift the pencil holder whenever it has to be moved. Place pens, pencils, and other long objects in the upper container, while the smaller one can be used for erasers, tweezers, and other such small objects — those that usually litter a desk and that would get lost in the bigger parallelepiped. To make this project, use a relatively heavy card, weighing between 200 and 250 gsm, and if preferred, with an interesting texture. The photographs present two examples: the one closest to the reader was made with green moonrock paper which, with its sponge-like surface, softens the lines of the holder. The one farthest away was made with a piece of stiff, compact cardboard, usually used for watercolors, that highlights the lines and the geometry of the whole model.

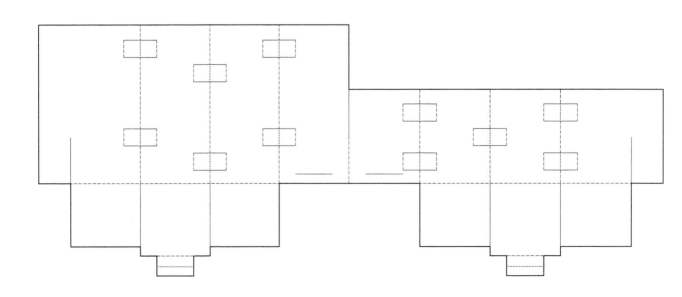

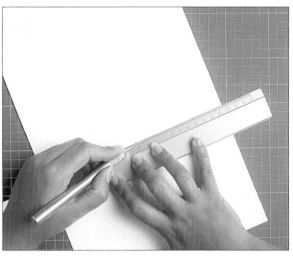

Enlarge the pattern by 285 percent. Cut out a 20 x 50 cm rectangle from the card you wish to use and secure it to the photocopy with a few strips of paper adhesive. To transfer the pattern, prick the ends of all the lines and margins with the point of a compass.

Score the mountain part of the folds with a cutter, checking on the pattern which dots are to be joined in this way. Turn the page over and repeat this operation for the folds with the mountain on the back. Use a metal ruler to get straight lines.

Cut the outline of the object and the inner lines that serve to create the indented parts of the model. Study the pattern to understand which holes are to be joined by a cutting line. Do not reverse steps 2 and 3; otherwise you risk not seeing the ends of the folding line.

Check that all the lines have been sharply cut, and start folding the bigger part of the model. First fold the longest valley folds slightly, parallel to each other, which creates the sides of the parallelepiped. Then fold the lines mountain-wise, pushing from the back part of the card with your fingers so as to obtain the indents in the photographs.

Remember always to work step-by-step so as to avoid putting too much pressure on the paper and to prevent additional folds from taking shape. When all the sides of this part have been properly folded, make the valley folds at the bottom, thus creating the base of the pencil holder. Now fold the tongue that will serve as the grip, mountain- and valley-wise.

Insert the tongue almost completely into the slit at the bottom, close to the smallest part of the object. You may encounter some difficulties if the paper is too thick. To avoid damaging the tongue by forcing it, run the cutter over the slit in order to widen it just that little bit extra.

Now insert the strip that protrudes from the outermost side into the slit between the two parts of the pencil holder. Bend this element slightly to help it slip in through the slit. This will prevent the object from opening by itself. If you should have difficulties in doing this, undo the tongue a little and start again.

Repeat the same folding operations, from the 4th to the 7th step for the smaller part of the model. When all the folding and slotting procedures are completed, check that the tongues which hold the object in place are all inserted well. Should they not be, pull them slightly until the mountain line coincides with the slit. Check that the base is flat inside as well, and complete the model.

FLOPPY DISK HOLDER

CUTTING DIFFICULTY*
FOLDING DIFFICULTY*
MATERIALS: 160 gsm LAVENDER AND GREEN CARDBOARD
DIMENSIONS: 12 X 25 cm SINGLE, 24 X 24 cm DOUBLE

MODEL: PAGE 158
TRACING: PAGE 24
CUTTING: PAGE 26
FOLDING: PAGE 28

The objects depicted in these pages have been designed for keeping and carrying your floppy disks so they won't be damaged. The disk holders, which can be made in either single or double versions, are also handy for cataloging your disks. As they are made of paper, you can write titles directly on them, and put notes or leave messages that are too long to write directly on the disk's label. At any rate, the label is still visible, even when the folder is closed. When full, these holders are light and can easily be carried in your pocket; when empty, they only take up the space of a square sheet of paper measuring 12 cm in width, and are therefore easy to store.

To make a folder, you will simply need a 160 gsm piece of card, and no glue or other type of adhesive. Both models are based on the asymmetrical 90-degree model with central valley fold. A tongue for closing the holder, once full, is added to this foundation sheet.

In the double model, a mountain fold between the two sections is also added.

This model does not require particularly difficult cuts or folds. Just copy the drawing, mark the folds, cut the card, and fold it so that four strips per disk emerge from the foundation sheet.

As can be seen in the photographs, in order to fill the holder one of the shorter side strips will need to be flattened; then the disk is inserted under the longer ones and last of all the previously flattened strip is raised up. In this way the disk will be held in on all sides and will not slip out on either side. In order to remove the disk, simply follow these instructions in reverse.

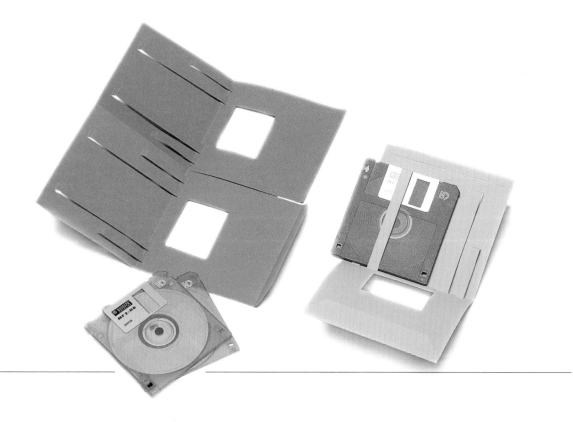

PHONE BOOK

CUTTING DIFFICULTY*
FOLDING DIFFICULTY**
MATERIALS: 90 gsm PARCHMENT PAPER
DIMENSIONS: 10 X 70 cm

MODEL: PAGE 158-159
TRACING: PAGE 24
CUTTING: PAGE 26
FOLDING: PAGE 27
DECORATING: PAGE 40

This phone book can be made from a single sheet of paper, neither glued nor bound. A simple cutting and folding system – similar to a concertina – will enable you to create a number of pages which you can then fill with addresses and telephone numbers. This system allows you to make the finished product without having to cut any section away. On opening the booklet, you see the letters from A to M, organized in pairs. On turning the book over, the remaining letters of the alphabet become visible.

Because the phone book is made from paper, you can write in any section of it, including the front and back covers — which could be used for your most important or most used numbers. The paper measurements chosen here are most suited to making a pocket phone book; by increasing these measurements your book could be used at home or at work. Use a fairly light paper, such as parchment paper, to ensure that the book remains fully flat once folded.

Cutting is fairly straightforward, while folding follows a repeated and simple valley-mountain-valley system. Before folding, decorate the sheet of paper by drawing (or, if you prefer, cutting out) the letters of the alphabet and by creasing the lines on which to write numbers and addresses. In order to do this, use the line folder for the drawing's thinnest lines, pressing hard so that the lines on the reverse side appear in relief. Then fold the model until flat, and place it under a heavy book for a while in order to make the folds permanent.

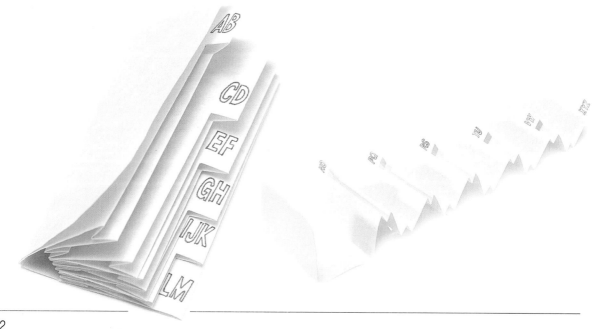

LAMP

CUTTING DIFFICULTY*
FOLDING DIFFICULTY**
MATERIALS: 200 gsm WATERCOLOR CARDBOARD
DIMENSIONS: 26 X 61 cm
LAMP STAND WITH BULB HOLDER

MODEL: PAGE 159
TRACING: PAGE 24
CUTTING: PAGE 26
FOLDING: PAGE 27

This model creates an atmosphere of light by using a sheet of cardboard and a metal stand. The cardboard is cut so as to keep it as distant as possible from the bulb (maximum 40 watts). This allows for air to pass between the bulb and card, and prevents the card from darkening or burning.

To make the model, use a piece of rigid and compact 200 gsm cardboard. Light or soft paper – such as handmade ones – would not hold the spacers that connect to the bulb bolder: they would bend and cause the paper to twist. If using handmade paper, do not use a stand, but place the cardboard directly on a surface instead. If you are following this option, you will need to buy a wire that has its own switch, plug, and bulb holder. Attach the spacers to the latter, and pass the wire through the cardboard's connecting strips. Cotton cards, especially those with natural inserts, will create attractive effects.

Follow this procedure when making the lamp: copy the model onto the card, pricking both ends of the lines with a compass; then mark the folds with the scoring technique and cut out the drawing that has been made. Now fold each side of the model and the central strips (which form the spacers), one by one. Slot the spacers between them and the edges of the card, so as to obtain the final shape. Unscrew the bulb holder's cap, attach the spacers, and screw the cap back on again so as to hold them in place. This procedure will allow you to create both types of lamp: the one with a stand and the one on the table.

ADVENT CALENDAR

CUTTING DIFFICULTY***
FOLDING DIFFICULTY***
MATERIALS: 160 gsm YELLOW AND BLUE CARDBOARD
DIMENSIONS: EACH 37 X 46 cm
YELLOW MARKER

The second group of objects found in this section is dedicated to Christmas. In the following pages you will find instructions that will allow you to make Advent calendars, place marks for dinner seating arrangements, and an angel-shaped decoration for the tree.

During December, while waiting for Christmas to arrive, many families hang a calendar with 25 numbered windows in their homes. Every day one of the windows is opened, to reveal a drawing, a hidden shape, or a chocolate.

Each window in the calendar presented in the following pages hides a small cardboard model. The overall structure is composed of two 160 gsm cards – one yellow and one blue – connected to each other by means of small tongues of card that slot into each window. The windows will open to form the shape of a Christmas tree on which, hypothetically, the figures in each window have been hung. For this reason, the small models will be shaped like spheres, presents, angels, or candles, and a star will glow from the highest point on the tree.

If this model is complicated, it is because it takes a long time to make and because you will need to handle small figures, rather than because each individual figure is difficult to cut and fold. The main folding systems are the symmetrical 90-degree one and, for windows 6, 9, 12, 14, 23, and 24, the asymmetrical 90-degree system. Follow these instructions step by step, and most of all be patient.

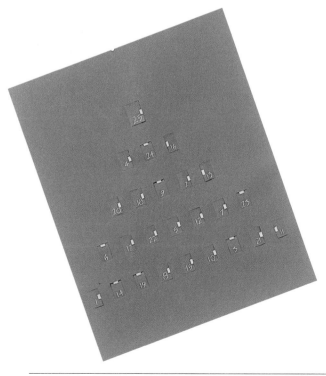

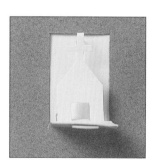
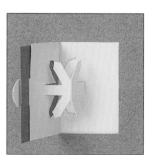

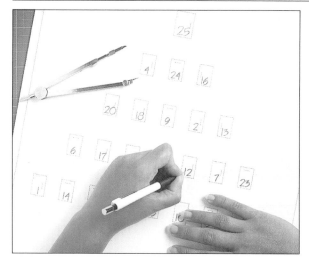

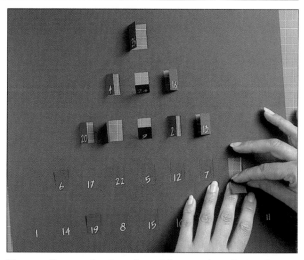

Enlarge the drawings of the calendar windows and of the main sheet with the small figures by 200 percent. Cut out a 37 x 46 cm rectangle from the blue cardboard and attach to it a sheet of graph paper and the drawing of the numbered windows. Prick and trace the figures and the numbers.

After having detached the card, mark the folds, mountain-side, with a cutter (note that in this model this is always on the reverse side of the card). Cut out the windows and the slots for the tongues of yellow cardboard.

Use a yellow marker to write out the numbers by tracing the marks left by the graph paper. Go over the numbers with the marker until they become clearly legible. Check that the windows have been cleanly cut and start folding them outward. The upper part of the calendar is now ready, to be used once the yellow cardboard has been cut and folded.

Now cut a 37 x 46 cm rectangle from the yellow cardboard. Using the same technique described above, trace the model. This is a fairly long operation, but try completing it with care and without rushing. Now mark the folds, and cut the cardboard by following the marks left by the graph paper. Be particularly careful with the snowflake in window number 10, with the angels and the star. Check that all figures have been cut properly by using the tip of the cutter, and make sure there are no corners that do not lift properly.

Erase the graph paper's remaining marks and start folding from the bottom row. Use a pair of tweezers to make this a little easier. Always start from the central valley fold and fold each figure as though it were a separate entity.

For the symmetrical models, first fold the two side valleys, one after the other, and then the central mountain one. Make sure you fold the central part inward when folding the star and the decorative spheres. Then move to the asymmetrical figures, such as the church, the manger, or the gifts.

Now complete the folding and ensure that all models fold back perfectly by forcibly flattening each window. Keep them flattened in this manner for a short while.

Lay the blue cardboard on the yellow, keeping each window open. Slot each sheet of cardboard into the other, ensuring that all the yellow tongues are inserted in the blue window slots as depicted in the photograph.

Once the two sheets of cardboard have been connected to each other, glue the external edges by inserting strips of double-sided tape between the sheets. Mark the center of the top part of the sheet with a pencil, then pierce it with a compass so as to be able to hang the calendar. If necessary, smooth the edges with a metal ruler and cutter. Complete the model by inserting all the yellow tongues under the blue cardboard so as to close each window.

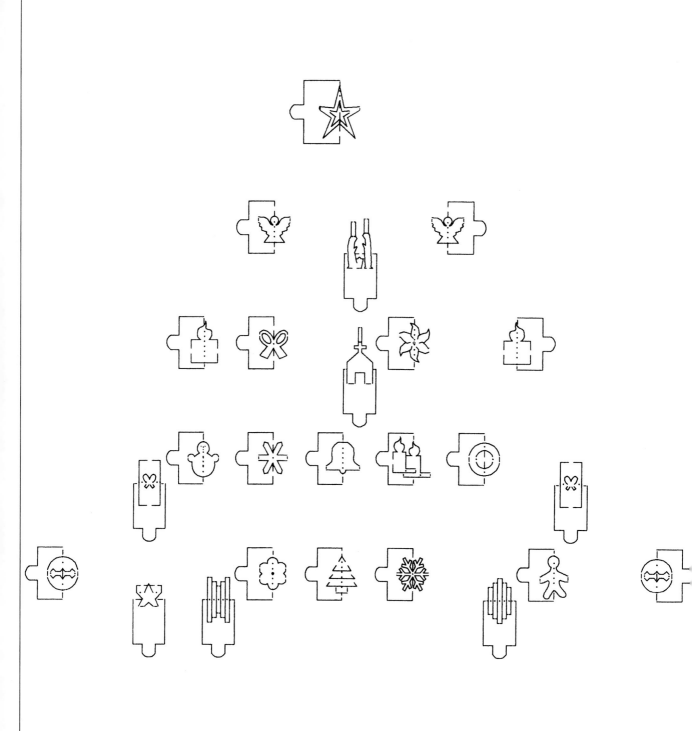

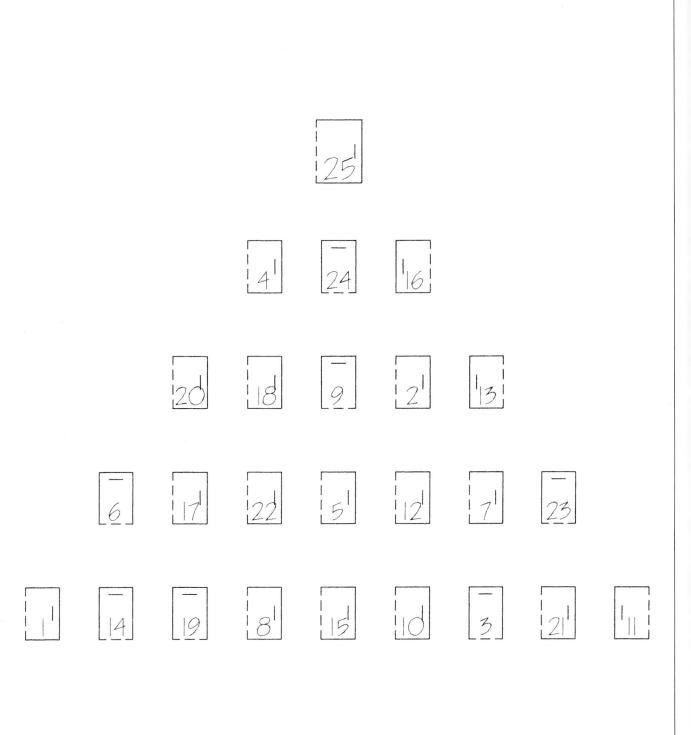

PLACE MARKS

CUTTING DIFFICULTY**
FOLDING DIFFICULTY*
MATERIALS: 160 gsm YELLOW AND GREEN CARDBOARD AND
COTTON PAPER WITH VEGETABLE FIBERS
SIZE: 7 X 9,5 cm GREEN AND YELLOW CARDBOARD;
3,5 X 6 cm COTTON CARDBOARD
MODEL: PAGE 157
TRACING: PAGE 24
CUTTING: PAGE 26
FOLDING: PAGE 27

These place marks enrich tables gaily set to celebrate Christmas and the New Year. The models can be made in any shape. The shapes chosen to make the models depicted on these pages are: Fir Trees and Stars, symbols usually associated with the Christmas season. You can alternate the two patterns on a dinner table, using different models for women and men.

This project is decidedly easy to make and requires a stiff cardboard for its structure and a softer one, such as cardboard with natural fibers, for the name tags. This last element is not necessary, but having it makes it possible to use this object again throughout the years. Once used, these place marks can be flattened, put aside when not needed, and used again the following year, merely by changing the name.

The structure of this model consists in two mountain folds and one valley fold. The star and the pine tree are obtained from the card by sectioning.

To increase the lightness and the three-dimensional effect, the subjects were tripled by layering: within a shape there is a smaller one, which has yet another one, and every one of them is slightly curved backward with respect to the preceding one.

After folding the model, all you need to do is place the name tag next to it. Use any kind of decorated paper.

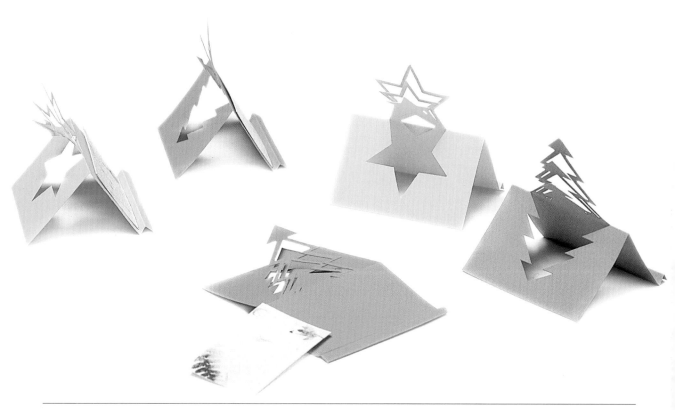

SMALL ANGELS

CUTTING DIFFICULTY**
FOLDING DIFFICULTY**
MATERIALS: 160 gsm RED CARDBOARD AND WATERCOLORS
DIMENSIONS: 9 X 11 cm EACH
GOLD TEMPERA

MODEL: PAGE 157
TRACING: PAGE 24
CUTTING: PAGE 26
FOLDING: PAGE 27
DECORATING: PAGE 36

Here is a simple decoration that can be used to enrich your Christmas trees. These white-and-red angels were obtained from a red sheet of 9 x 11 cm paper and spray-decorated with gold tempera color.

To hang them to the branches, thread a light string through the small hole next to the angel's hairlock. As with the previous projects, these characters can also be flattened so as to occupy as little space as possible when they are not used. In order to preserve the models throughout the years, store them away from dust and direct sunlight.

This model is quite quick to make and not difficult to cut or fold. It is made up mainly of curved lines that should be cut without haste, taking care not to remove the cutter from the sheet of paper. Should this prove difficult, try using a slightly lighter cardboard and turning the paper instead of moving the cutter. Remember to score the mountain part of the folds with a cutter; by doing so, all you need to do is pinch the model slightly into place. Once folded, lift the angel's nose with the tip of the cutter and widen his eyes a little if you think it necessary.

Now decorate the model with one or more colors according to the type of cardboard you have chosen. The examples depicted on these pages were made using white and red cardboard and were then sprayed lightly with gold tempera, to highlight them against the green branches from which they'll hang.

STAGE THEATER

CUTTING DIFFICULTY***
FOLDING DIFFICULTY**
MATERIALS: 250 gsm RED CARDBOARD,
160 gsm WHITE CARDBOARD,
AND WATERCOLOR CARDBOARD
DIMENSIONS: 36 X 70 cm RED CARDBOARD,
10 X 30 cm WHITE CARDBOARD,
12 X 30 CM WATERCOLOR CARDBOARD
WATERCOLORS

The last group of objects consists of two games: the theater and masks. The former is a game to be invented, changing the characters and the stage set each time and telling ever different stories. The latter is an object that can be sported to become a cat or a rabbit.

The fairy-tale world fascinates children of all ages. Story-telling stimulates children's imagination and can be highly educational, as well as purely enjoyable. A theater with ever-changing backgrounds and characters thus becomes the perfect object for imaginative playing. In the examples depicted on these pages are the sets and characters from the tale of Little Red Riding Hood, but this is only one of the possibilities available. With a little imagination it will be possible to invent new stories, letting the children draw and color the backgrounds and the characters themselves, perhaps with techniques that do not require a cutter. Once the children have finished playing, the theater can be folded in such a way as to take up the space of a sheet of paper, and all the sets and actors can be put away in a pocket underneath the stage. In this way, the game can be kept and carried with ease. All you need to do is reopen the stage tunnel-manner and take out the elements from the pocket to find yourself at the theater once more. You can always make new characters for new plays.

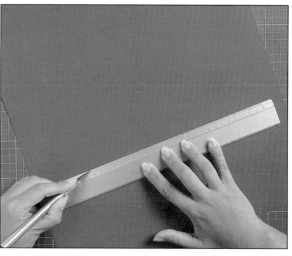

Enlarge the pattern of the 3 objects by 275 percent: the theater, the sets, and the characters. Cut a 36 x 79 cm rectangle from the red cardboard and trace onto it the pattern of the theater, made up of the tunnel and, on the opposite side, the valley fold. Mark the folds with the point of the compass.

Remove the pattern from the cardboard and score the mountain part of the folds with a cutter, joining the previously made holes with the compass. Check which folds should be mountain and which valley.

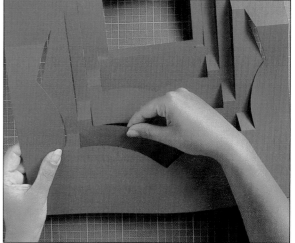

Start by cutting the curtain curves. Then cut the straight lines with a metal ruler, beginning with the innermost lines. Remove the rectangle forming the stage's background and check that everything has been cut properly.

Fold the theater's tunnel structure by following the instructions on page 30. Now fold the valley on the opposite side of the cardboard. Glue the side edges of the theater to the section folded valley-wise, so as to create a fold underneath the stage.

Now take the 12 x 30 cm rectangle cut from the watercolor card. Trace the two backdrops and the drawing of the shrub that is placed between them by using a photocopier. Cut out the resulting drawings.

Glue the shrub to the right-hand side of the set by the house and trees. Now decorate the two backdrops with your favorite technique; in this example we have used light watercolors.

Once the two sheets of cardboard have dried, try inserting them into the theater by using the gap between the back level and the second to last. Check that the foundations are not bent when the theater is open. Should this occur, straighten them with your hands and place them for a while under a heavy object.

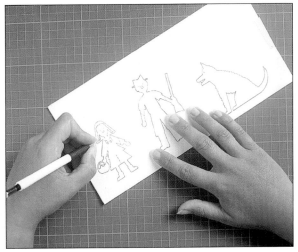

Next, trace the drawing of the three people on a sheet of 160 gsm white cardboard. Avoid using heavier cardboard, as this would make cutting the curved lines difficult. Then lift the drawing off the cardboard.

Cut out Little Red Riding Hood, the wolf, and the hunter. Lift the three characters off the sheet of paper and check that the girl's ribbon, as well as the girl's and hunter's noses, are properly cut out. Prepare three small stands by cutting 0.5 x 30 cm strips of watercolor card.

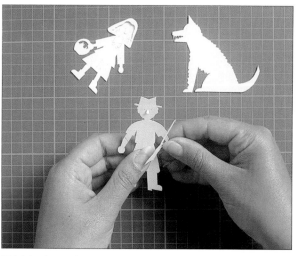

Fold the hunter's arms by following the two valley lines on the drawing, and slightly bend the nose forward by lifting it with the cutter. Repeat this operation for Little Red Riding Hood's nose and ribbon, then fold her arm and skirt as shown.

Decorate the figures with watercolors. In this example, the wolf's paws, tail, and ears are tinted brown; Little Red Riding Hood has black boots and a red ribbon, nose, and apples; the hunter's gun is brown, his hat and boots green.

Once the figures have dried, glue a stand to the back of each, deciding whether to fix them on sideways or facing upward. In the first instance the character will enter and exit the stage from the sides, in the second it will rise and fall from above.

MASKS

CUTTING DIFFICULTY***
FOLDING DIFFICULTY**
MATERIALS: 220 gsm LIGHT BLUE AND ORANGE CARDBOARD
DIMENSIONS: LIGHT BLUE, MAX. 26 X 32 cm;
ORANGE MAX. 26 X 26 cm

MODEL: PAGE 160
TRACING: PAGE 24
CUTTING: PAGE 26
FOLDING: PAGE 27

To end with, here are two carnival masks: Slykit and Robbyrabbit. Both are made with only one sheet of cardboard and can be worn by threading a string through the side holes. In order to keep them in good condition, fold them up as shown in the photographs; they will not take up much space and will be in a fit condition to be used again and again.

Enlarge the drawings to fit the face of the person who will be wearing the mask, paying particular attention to the distance between eyes and nose. The maximum measurements listed above are appropriate to an enlargement of 200 percent, suitable for an adult's face. 200-250gsm card is the most suitable for this model. Do not use a lightweight paper as some parts, such as the rabbit's ears, would fold; nor one that is too thick, as the whisker tips could become a little too sharp. Watercolor paper is also suitable, especially if decorated with bright colors. To stop the whisker tips from curling, follow the instructions on page 34.

Remember to mark the folds with the scoring technique and, once you have cut the figures out, fold the models, by starting from the center. To fold the nose, use your finger to push from behind so as to lift the whole of the valley-mountain-valley section converging on the central fold. As always, remember to fold gradually, so as to obtain the end result without having to push the card too far.

DRAWINGS

This section offers the drawings needed to make all the models described in this book. Those models which have been described step-by-step are not illustrated here; those drawings may be found with their instructions. To make the models described in this book, you will need to use cardboard of differing sizes. The most common is a 15 x 20 cm rectangle. Folded in two, it becomes the size of a postcard and is therefore small enough to fit in your pocket or to be posted. Next to each diagram you will find a number representing the reproduction scale. There are three main types of scale: if the drawing is reproduced in the book to its own scale, it will be captioned "copy at 100%"; if it is three-quarters its real size, it will be captioned "enlarge by 133%"; and if the drawing is half its real size, it will be captioned with "enlarge by 200%". Simply photocopy or, if you prefer, pantograph the drawings in accordance with these scales and you will have a correct-sized model ready for you to use. Your imagination will, at a second stage, tell you whether you would prefer the model to be larger or smaller than that suggested — in which case you can adjust the scale of the copies accordingly. Also remember that you will find three types of line in the drawings:

———————— cutting line

----------- valley fold

.... mountain fold

In wishing you a happy and enjoyable time, we leave you with one last bit of advice. Each time you try out a new model, closely observe the related photographs and follow the explanations found in this book; they will provide you with invaluable assistance.

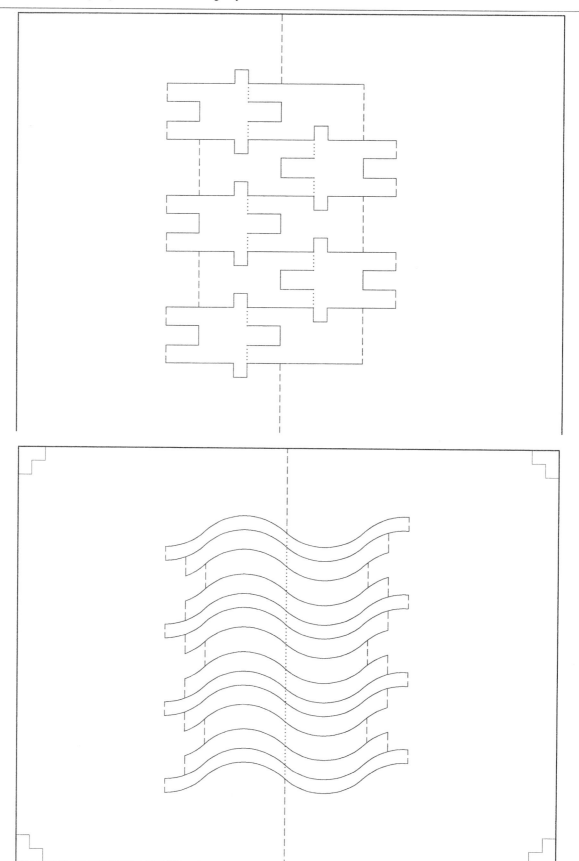

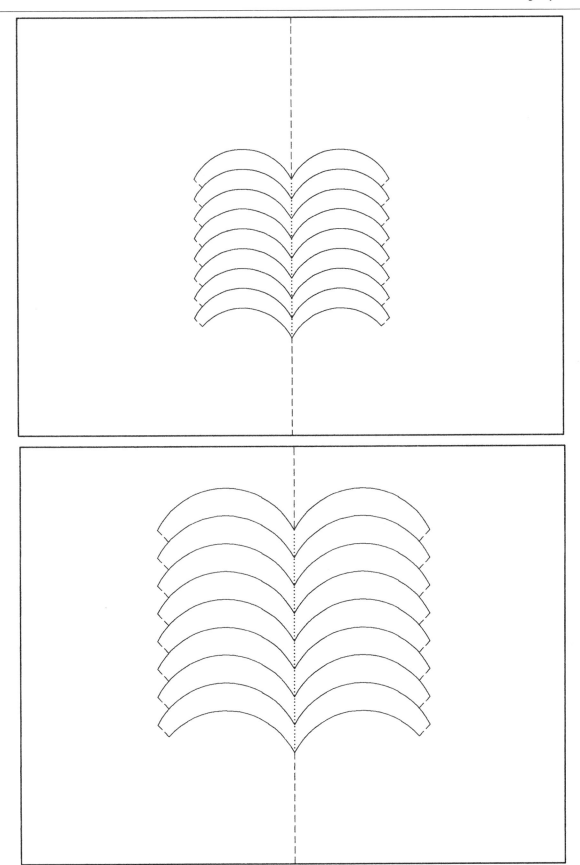

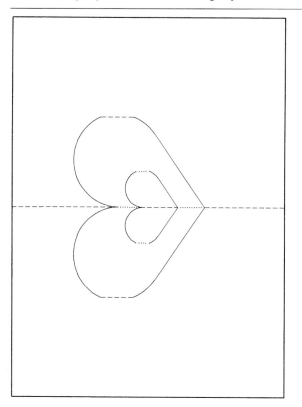

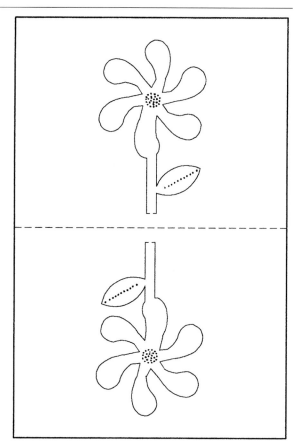

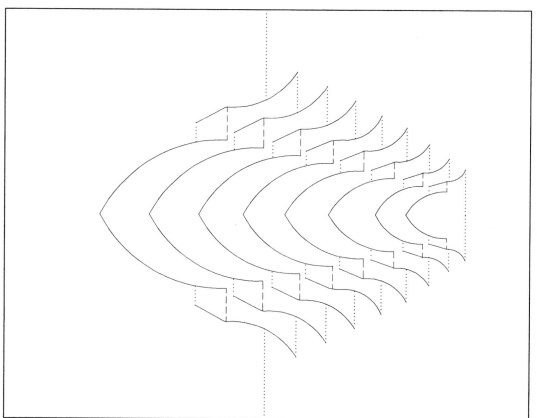

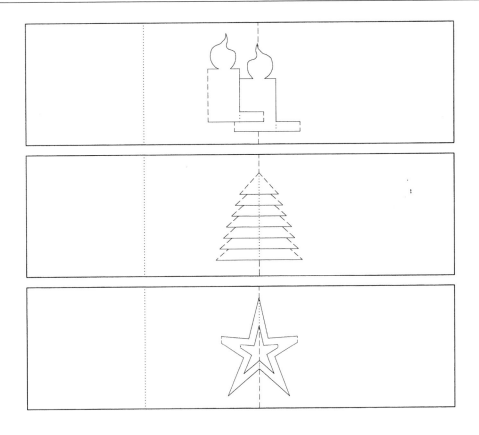

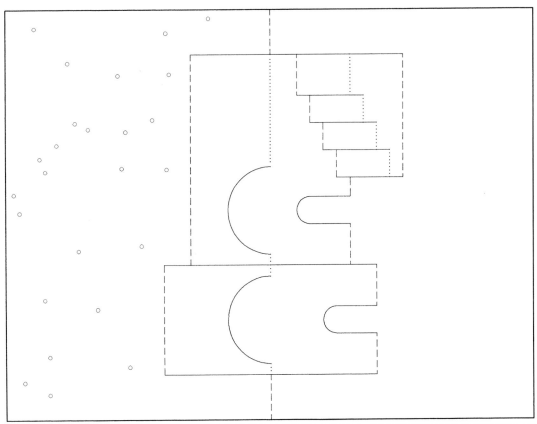

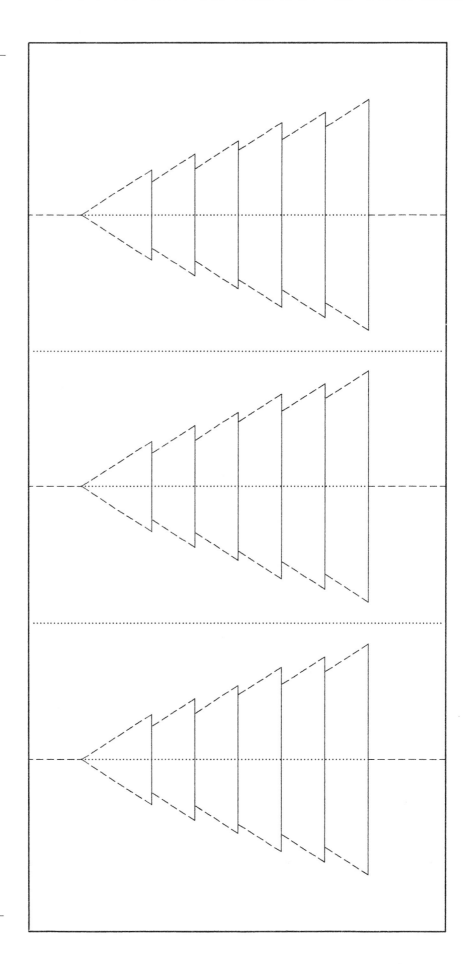

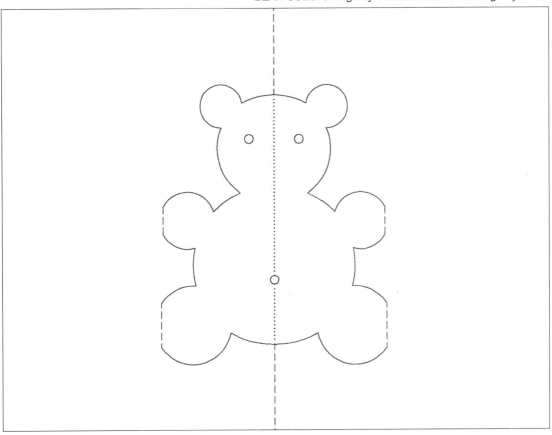

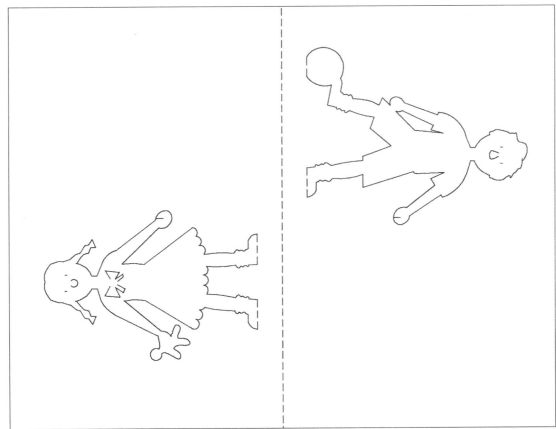

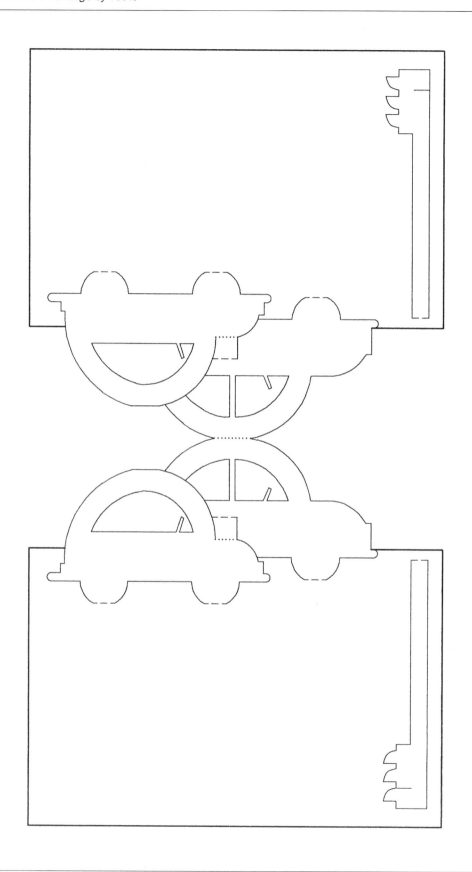

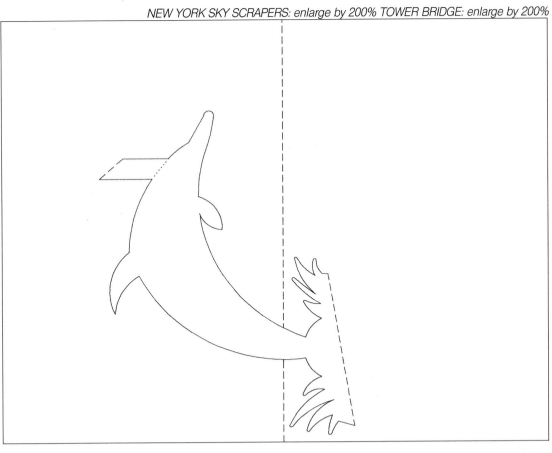

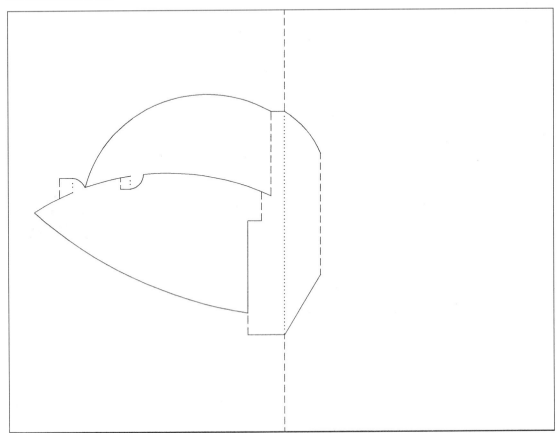

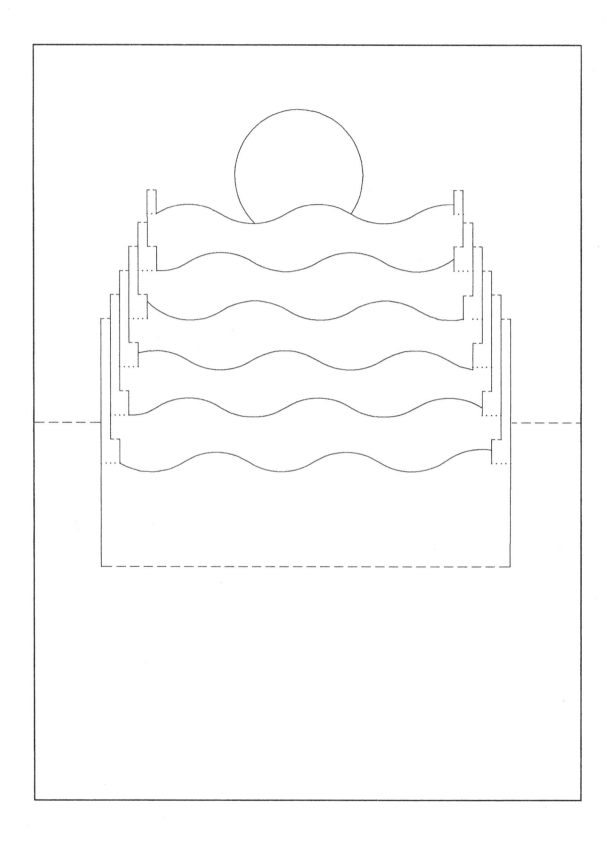

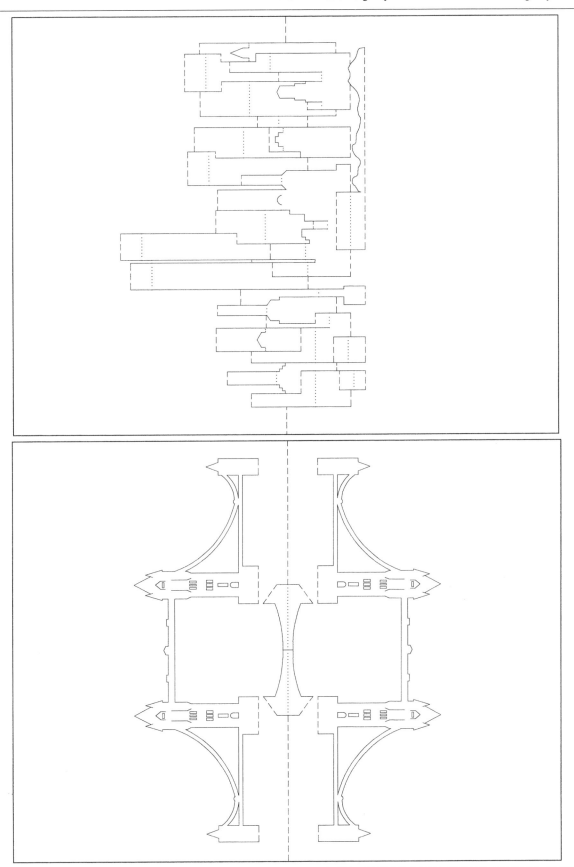

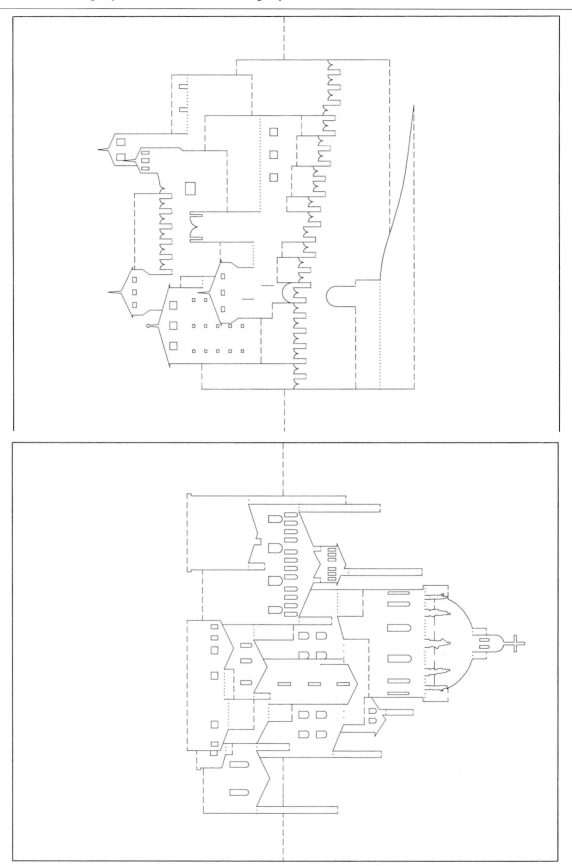

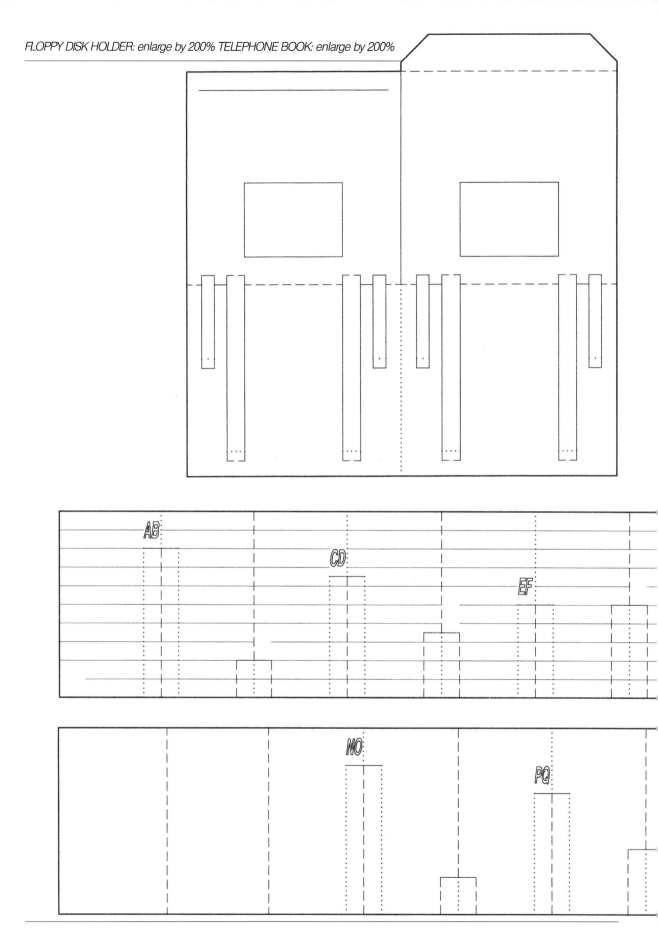

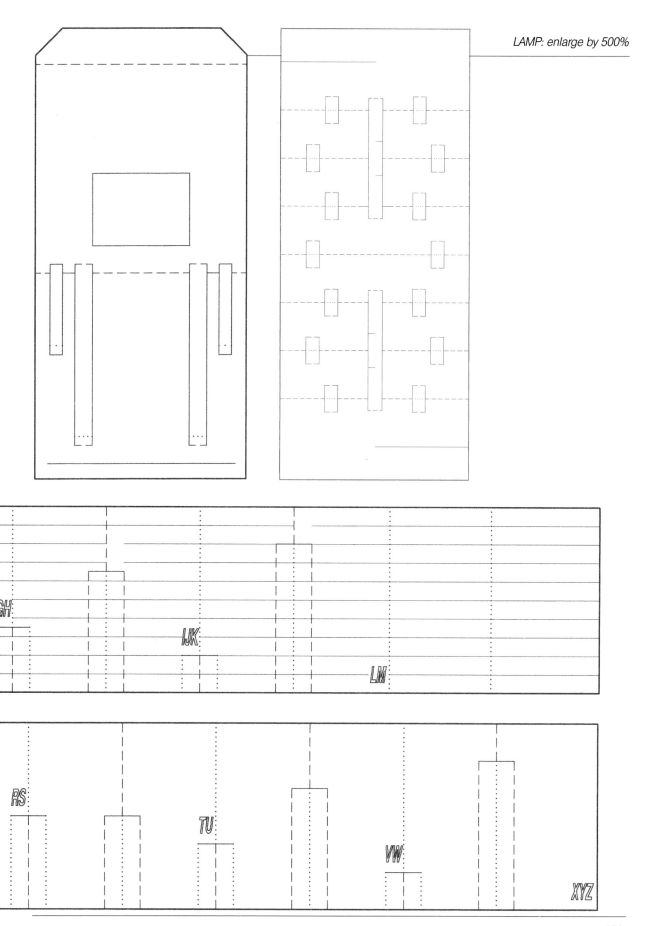

LAMP: enlarge by 500%

MASKS: enlarge by 200%